CAMPAIGN • 245

DEMYANSK 1942–43

The frozen fortress

ROBERT FORCZYK

ILLUSTRATED BY PETER DENNIS

Series editor Marcus Cowper

First published in Great Britain in 2012 by Osprey Publishing,
Midland House, West Way, Botley, Oxford OX2 0PH, UK
44-02 23rd St, Suite 219, Long Island City, NY 11101, USA

E-mail: info@ospreypublishing.com

© 2012 Osprey Publishing Ltd

OSPREY PUBLISHING IS PART OF THE OSPREY GROUP

A CIP catalogue record for this book is available from the British Library.

ISBN: 978 1 84908 552 6

Editorial by Ilios Publishing Ltd, Oxford, UK (www.iliospublishing.com)
Page layout by: The Black Spot
Index by Sharon Redmayne
Typeset in Sabon and Myriad Pro
Maps by Bounford.com
3D bird's-eye view by The Black Spot
Battlescene illustrations by Peter Dennis
Originated by Blenheim Colour Ltd, Oxford
Printed in China through Worldprint

12 13 14 15 16 10 9 8 7 6 5 4 3 2 1

ARTIST'S NOTE

Readers may care to note that the original paintings from which the colour
plates in this book were prepared are available for private sale. The
Publishers retain all reproduction copyright whatsoever. All enquiries
should be addressed to:

Peter Dennis, Fieldhead, the Park, Mansfield, NOTTS, NG18 2AT, UK

Email: magie.h@ntlworld.com

The Publishers regret that they can enter into no correspondence
upon this matter.

DEDICATION

In remembrance of Capt. Waid C. Ramsey, HHC, 1st Battalion, 20th Special
Forces Group (Airborne), killed by hostile small arms fire in Paktika Province,
Afghanistan, 4 August 2011.

ACKNOWLEDGEMENTS

I wish to thank Phil Curme, Nik Cornish, Ian Barter, Ralph Gibson of RIA
Novosti and the staff of the Bundesarchiv for their help with this project.

GLOSSARY

AOK – Armeeoberkommando (Army)

GRC – Guards Rifle Corps

GRD – Guards Rifle Division

OKH – Oberkommando des Heeres

Key to military symbols

xxxxx	Army Group
xxxx	Army
xxx	Corps
xx	Division
x	Brigade
III	Regiment
II	Battalion
I	Company/Battery
•••	Platoon
••	Section
•	Squad
	Infantry
	Artillery
	Cavalry
	Airborne
	Unit HQ
	Air defence
	Air Force
	Air mobile
	Air transportable
	Amphibious
	Anti-tank
	Armour
	Air aviation
	Bridging
	Engineer
	Headquarters
	Maintenance
	Medical
	Missile
	Mountain
	Navy
	Nuclear, biological, chemical
	Ordnance
	Parachute
	Reconnaissance
	Signal
	Supply
	Transport movement
	Rocket artillery
	Air defence artillery

Key to unit identification

Unit identifier / Parent unit / Commander
(+) with added elements
(–) less elements

CONTENTS

Situation, right wing of Heeresgruppe Nord, 6 January 1942

1   189. Infanterie-Regiment (81 ID) arrives by train from France at
    Andreapol on 5 January.
2   18. Infanterie-Division (mot.) redeploying from Tikhvin to serve as
    AOK 16 reserve force.
3   290. Infanterie-Division is defending a nearly 30-mile-wide (50km)
    sector along the Pola River with only company-sized
    strongpoints.
4   123. Infanterie-Division screens the right flank of AOK 16 across a
    35-mile-wide (55km) sector.
5   The reconnaissance battalion from SS-Kavallerie-Brigade screens
    the left flank of Heeresgruppe Mitte near Peno.
6   281. Sicherungs-Division has various units operating against
    Russian partisans around Kholm.

INTRODUCTION

German infantry advance into a village south of Lake Il'men in August 1941. Initially, AOK 16 planned on only transiting through this region en route to the Valdai Hills but was forced onto the defensive by a series of Soviet counterattacks around Staraya Russa that encircled part of X Armeekorps (AK) for a week. (Ian Barter)

Although the original plan for Operation *Barbarossa* developed in late 1940 had specified Leningrad and Moscow as critical objectives, it had provided no real guidance about the heavily forested and lake-strewn region that lay between the two cities. Aside from the ancient Russian capital of Novgorod, there was little of strategic value in the area around the Valdai Hills except the main Moscow–Leningrad railway line. Both Hitler and the German Oberkommando des Heeres (OKH) simply assumed that intermediary areas such as these would easily fall into the Wehrmacht's hands once the Red Army was crushed in the opening stages of *Barbarossa*. Nor did the OKH anticipate positional warfare in the vast and remote areas of northern Russia, but instead believed that rapid manoeuvre warfare would compensate for lack of sufficient forces to create a continuous front.

By October 1941, the German troops in AOK 16 were settled into a defensive posture and had plenty of time to build field fortifications. This higher level of preparedness was a major advantage in surviving the Soviet Winter Counteroffensive and holding the Demyansk salient for the rest of 1942. (Ian Barter)

When the German invasion began on 22 June 1941, the Soviet North-western Front had 440,000 troops deployed with its 8th and 11th Armies on the border in Lithuania and with 27th Army in Latvia. Caught totally by surprise, the two Soviet armies on the border suffered 20 per cent losses in personnel in the first 18 days of the invasion and were forced to retreat 375 miles (600km) across the Baltic States. Forced apart by the German Panzer *Schwerpunkt*, 8th Army withdrew towards Narva, while 11th Army fell back towards Staraya Russa and 27th Army towards Kholm. The bulk of Heeresgruppe Nord under Generalfeldmarschall Wilhelm Ritter von Leeb advanced towards Leningrad, leaving only 16. Armee (AOK 16) under Generaloberst Ernst Busch to guard the right flank of the army group. By mid-July, X Armeekorps (AK) was pushing towards Staraya Russa while II AK advanced slowly upon the town of Kholm. Both Leeb and the OKH viewed the AOK 16 mission as an economy of force effort, accomplished with the bare minimum of forces and supplies diverted from the main objective of Leningrad.

However, the North-western Front was not annihilated in the first two months of the German invasion – despite horrendous losses, particularly in tanks and artillery – and it soon became apparent that the Wehrmacht had invaded the Soviet Union with grossly insufficient forces for such a mammoth task. While powerful Panzer *Schwerpunkte* pushed rapidly towards the prizes in Moscow and Leningrad, Heeresgruppe Nord and Heeresgruppe Mitte had only tenuous contact with each other. Once out of harm's way, the Soviet 11th Army stopped retreating when it reached the area of swamps and forests south of Lake Il'men, knowing that the road-bound Germans could not easily pursue them in this terrain. After catching its breath and receiving reinforcements, the North-western Front began launching a series of painful counterattacks that kept catching AOK 16 by surprise. On 15 July 1941, the Soviet 11th Army counterattacked west of Lake Il'men and was able briefly to encircle and maul 8. Panzer-Division at the battle of Soltsy. As a result, Generalfeldmarschall von Leeb became very concerned about his vulnerable right flank and decided to order AOK 16 to secure a defensible line along the Lovat River. As a result, in early August 1941, X AK seized Staraya Russa while II AK occupied Kholm.

Despite securing these towns, which were vital transportation hubs in a nearly roadless region, Generaloberst Busch did not have sufficient forces to create a continuous front between Staraya Russa and Kholm. It was not long before the North-western Front decided to take advantage of the 30-mile-wide (48km) gap between the two German corps. While 11th Army conducted a fixing attack against X AK at Staraya Russa on 12 August, the newly raised 34th Army pushed into the gap and was able to sever the main German lines of communication. Two German divisions – 30. and 290. Infanterie-Divisionen – were briefly surrounded in Staraya Russa until Leeb sent General der Infanterie Erich von Manstein's LVI AK (mot.), spearheaded by SS-'Totenkopf' Division, to relieve the trapped forces at Staraya Russa. In less than a week, Manstein was able to punch through the thin Soviet encirclement and crush the overextended 34th Army. The North-western Front retreated back across the Lovat River, to regroup.

The battle for Staraya Russa in August 1941 shaped the forthcoming Demyansk–Kholm campaign of 1942, as constant Soviet attacks from the Valdai Hills region enticed AOK 16 to keep pushing ever farther eastward, past the relative safety of the Lovat River line. Stung by this second, nearly successful Soviet counterattack, Leeb resolved to ensure that his right flank was secure before beginning the final push on Leningrad. He ordered Manstein's corps to remain with AOK 16 and continue pushing eastward across the Lovat River, rather than supporting the drive on Leningrad. Given that the priority for Soviet reinforcements was Moscow and Leningrad, there was little that the weakened North-western Front could do to stop AOK 16 from slowly pushing the mauled 34th Army back towards Demyansk, although 11th Army and 27th Army held firm on the flanks. Manstein's LVI AK (mot.) was able to advance down a narrow road through the swamps east of the Lovat River and capture the town of Demyansk in early September, but the result was that a handful of German divisions were now overextended and vulnerable to counterattack. Indeed, the idea that an entire army corps with three divisions would place its main supply route on a single 55-mile-long (90km) dirt road from the railhead at Staraya Russa was not only at odds with German manoeuvre doctrine but bordered on the ludicrous.

Soviet KV-1 tanks and infantry attack through flooded marshland near Staraya Russa in the autumn of 1941. The North-western Front continued to conduct small-scale attacks against AOK 16's positions throughout the rest of 1941, but heavy tanks proved almost useless in this kind of terrain. (Phil Curme)

German troops moving through marshy, forested terrain near Staraya Russa. The Wehrmacht was unaccustomed to operating in the type of terrain prevalent south of Lake Il'men, which favoured light infantry units and partisans, rather than mechanized divisions. (Ian Barter)

In early September, LVI AK (mot.) was withdrawn to reinforce Operation *Typhoon* against Moscow, but SS-'Totenkopf' remained with X AK. Before X AK could establish a strong defence, the North-western Front struck again on 24 September, catching SS-'Totenkopf' by surprise at the village of Luzhno, 12 miles (20km) north of Demyansk. The Waffen-SS Division was pounded for three days and suffered over 800 casualties, but held. As October arrived, AOK 16 made one last effort to push east from Demyansk and Staraya Russa, but succeeded only in seizing more barren wilderness that was difficult to defend. Once the first snow arrived, the on-again/off-again AOK 16 offensive came to a halt and Busch ordered all three of his corps to construct winter defences. Busch had XXXVIII AK defending the area north of Lake Il'men, including Novgorod, with X AK holding the area east of Staraya Russa and II AK holding the area between Demyansk and Ostashkov. Over the next two months, a period of stalemate settled over the area between Lake Il'men and Lake Seliger. Since the North-western Front had suffered 178,000 casualties between 10 July and the end of December 1941, it was in no position immediately to take advantage of the German shift to a defensive posture. Enjoying the respite from Soviet counterattacks, AOK 16 dug in and waited for the campaign to be decided elsewhere, at Leningrad and Moscow. Although AOK 16's lines were thin and the connection with Heeresgruppe Mitte's left flank was tenuous, the OKH assumed this to be a temporary but acceptable risk.

However when the German advances upon Leningrad and then Moscow were stopped short of their objectives, it became apparent that the risk in AOK 16's sector would not be temporary. Operation *Barbarossa* had barely culminated when the Soviet Winter Counteroffensive began, first in front of Moscow and then at Tikhvin, east of Leningrad. Initially, AOK 16 was not affected by these actions and December passed fairly quietly on this front. The 290. Infanterie-Division, holding the most exposed section of the X AK sector, suffered a total of only 127 combat casualties in December. Indeed, this barren wilderness appeared to be just about the only quiet section on the entire Eastern Front, as virtually every other German army was stressed by the Soviet counteroffensives. Nor did AOK 16 suffer as severely from the cold as other German troops in Russia did, since its units had sufficient time to build fieldworks and plenty of timber for bunkers. As the Germans had already discovered, the terrain in this region favoured the defence and Busch was confident that AOK 16 could hold its ground through the winter. The only area of real concern was at the inter-army group boundary on the right flank, near Ostashkov and Lake Seliger. Throughout the 1941 campaign, the connection between Heeresgruppe Nord and Heeresgruppe Mitte had been poor and recurrent Soviet counteroffensives from the Valdai Hills only made it worse. The OKH also recognized that this area was potentially quite dangerous and promised Busch reinforcements. Even though Heeresgruppe Mitte was in full retreat from Moscow and Soviet offensives were appearing across the front, the OKH was transferring a number of units from occupation duty in France and promised Busch 81. Infanterie-Division. When the first elements of this division began arriving by rail at the end of December, Busch sent a *Kampfgruppe* composed of Infanterie-Regiment 189 and an artillery battalion to reinforce his right flank, but directed the rest of the division to concentrate around Staraya Russa. He also received the badly depleted 18. Infanterie-Division (mot.) from AOK 18 at Leningrad.

From the Soviet perspective, the area south of Lake Il'men initially seemed to offer merely a cost-effective venue for diverting German reserves away from Leningrad and Moscow. Yet as the Soviet Winter Counteroffensive gathered momentum, the Stavka recognized that the poorly guarded boundary between Heeresgruppe Nord and Heeresgruppe Mitte could be exploited to shatter the entire German front in northern Russia. Consequently, in late December the Stavka began funnelling fresh reinforcements and replacements to enable the North-western Front to mount a major attack against AOK 16 in January 1942. Stalin was confident that this forthcoming operation could cripple both German army groups and lead to decisive results.

CHRONOLOGY

1941

6 August — AOK 16 captures Staraya Russa and Kholm.

12 August — Soviet 11th and 34th Armies attack X AK at Staraya Russa and isolate two German divisions.

19 August — Manstein counterattacks with LVI AK (mot.) and rescues X AK.

31 August — Demyansk captured by LVI AK (mot.).

24–27 September — Soviet attacks against SS-'Totenkopf' Division at Luzhno are repulsed.

29 September — First German supply train arrives in Staraya Russa.

8–19 October — AOK 16 briefly renews advance eastwards to improve its positions.

18 December — North-western Front receives order from Stavka to begin planning for the Winter Counteroffensive.

1942

6–7 January — Winter Counteroffensive by North-western Front against 16 AOK begins.

9 January — 3th and 4th Shock Armies begin attacks across frozen Lake Seliger, striking right flank of AOK 16.

11 January — 11th Army severs the main supply route to Demyansk.

12 January — Leeb requests permission to pull back II and X AK, but Hitler refuses.

15 January — 4th Shock Army breaks through at Andreapol.

17 January — Leeb is relieved and replaced by Küchler.

19 January — The Germans rush LIX AK to Vitebsk to plug hole between Heeresgruppe Nord and Heeresgruppe Mitte.

20 January — 11th Army attacks Staraya Russa while 4th Shock Army overruns supply depot at Toropets. Primary land communications with II AK are severed.

21 January — 3rd Shock Army surrounds Kampfgruppe Scherer at Kholm.

22 January — 3rd and 4th Shock Armies transferred to Kalinin Front.

22–25 January — Heavy fighting at Kholm.

29 January — 1st GRC arrives at front east of Staraya Russa.

3 February — 2nd GRC committed at Staraya Russa.

8 February	1st GRC captures Ramushevo on the Lovat.	**22 April**	First supplies reach Demyansk through the corridor.
12 February	Luftflotte 1 begins airlift to Demyansk pocket.	**3–17 May**	First Soviet offensive against Ramushevo corridor.
8–13 February	1st Shock Army committed south of Staraya Russa.	**5 May**	XXXIX Panzerkorps breaks through 3rd Shock Army to relieve Kholm.
15–18 February	A Soviet airborne battalion parachutes inside the Demyansk pocket.	**17–24 July**	Second Soviet offensive against Ramushevo corridor.
22 February	Hitler declares Demyansk a *Festung*.	**10–21 August**	Third Soviet offensive against Ramushevo corridor.
25 February	1st GRC and Group Ksenofontov link up, thereby isolating II AK in the Demyansk pocket.	**27 September to 5 October**	German *Michael* counteroffensive widens Ramushevo corridor.
2 March	Hitler approves Operation *Brückenschlag* to relieve Demyansk pocket.	**17 November**	Timoshenko takes command of North-western Front.
6 March	Soviet 1st Airborne Corps begins infiltration attack into Demyansk pocket.	**28 November to 12 January**	Fourth Soviet offensive against Ramushevo corridor.
		1943	
18 March	34th Army and a parachute brigade launch a coordinated attack on Lychkovo, but are repulsed.	**31 January**	Hitler authorizes evacuation of Demyansk salient.
19 March	Soviet paratroopers conduct a raid on the Demyansk airfields but are repulsed.	**15 February**	Fifth Soviet offensive against Ramushevo corridor.
		17 February	The Germans begin evacuation of Demyansk salient.
21 March	Korpsgruppe Seydlitz begin relief Operation *Brückenschlag*.	**28 February**	German evacuation of the salient is complete.
14 April	Korpsgruppe Zorn launches Operation *Fallreep* to break out towards relief force.	**1944**	
21 April	Seydlitz's relief force links up with SS-'Totenkopf' near Ramushevo.	**21 February**	Kholm liberated by Red Army.

OPPOSING COMMANDERS

GERMAN

The commander of Heeresgruppe Nord during the Demyansk–Kholm campaign was initially Generalfeldmarschall Wilhelm Ritter von Leeb but he was soon succeeded by Generalfeldmarschall Georg Wilhelm von Küchler. Both commanders gave the priority of their attention to operations around Leningrad and tended to delegate much of the operational responsibility to Generaloberst Ernst Busch. The German commanders in the Demyansk–Kholm campaign were not as well known as their peers on other fronts, but they were equally effective. It is important to note that despite being faced with a near-catastrophic situation, the leaders in AOK 16 demonstrated an ability to recover from setbacks that made the German Army so tenacious in defence in World War II.

Generaloberst Ernst Busch (1885–1945), commander of AOK 16 from January 1940. He was tasked with holding the difficult right flank of Heeresgruppe Nord, extending from Staraya Russa to Ostashkov. Busch first entered the Prussian Army in 1904 and served as an infantry company commander and battalion commander on the Western Front in 1918. He particularly distinguished himself in combat in Champagne in 1918, for which he received the Pour le Mérite. Busch was retained in the post-war Reichswehr and received General Staff training. Perceived by some as pro-Nazi, Busch rose rapidly once Hitler came to power, becoming a division commander in 1935 and a corps commander in 1938. He led VIII AK in southern Poland in 1939 and then AOK 16 against the French Maginot Line in 1940. Busch was a solid, if not terribly imaginative, commander.

General der Infanterie Walter Graf von Brockdorff-Ahlefeldt (1887–1943), commander of II AK inside the Demyansk pocket. He commanded II AK from 21 June 1940 until 28 November 1942. After entering the army in 1908, Brockdorff-Ahlefeldt served in World War I and was badly wounded as an infantry company commander at Verdun in 1916. Like Busch, he was retained in the Reichswehr and trained as a General Staff officer. He succeeded Busch as commander of 23. Infanterie-Division in 1938 and led this formation in the Polish and French campaigns. During the early stages of *Barbarossa*, he was awarded the Ritterkreuz der Eisernes Kreuz for his capture of Kovno. Like many Wehrmacht officers in Russia, Brockdorff-Ahlefeldt became ill during the winter of 1941–42 and was not at his best during the early phase of the encirclement battle. Nevertheless, Brockdorff-

LEFT
Generaloberst Ernst Busch found the bulk of his AOK 16 either surrounded or hard pressed by near-encirclement by the end of February 1942. Despite this, he proved to be a solid commander in adversity and was rewarded for his steadfast leadership after the Demyansk campaign by promotion to *Generalfeldmarschall* and command of Heeresgruppe Mitte. However, he was still in command when the Soviet *Bagration* offensive obliterated Heeresgruppe Mitte in June 1944 and Hitler relieved him. (Author's collection)

CENTRE
General der Infanterie Walter Graf von Brockdorff-Ahlefeldt, commander of II AK for the bulk of the Demyansk Campaign. (Author's collection)

RIGHT
General der Artillerie Christian Hansen, commander of X AK, underestimated the Soviet ability to manoeuvre through frozen marshes and over icy lakes and, consequently, was surprised by the enemy breakthrough in January 1942. However, he recovered from his error and orchestrated a stubborn defence of Staraya Russa that held off all Soviet attacks and thereby determined the outcome of the campaign. (Bundesarchiv, Bild 146-1971-035-88)

Ahlefeldt's calm leadership during the worst days of the siege helped to maintain morale. His illness persisted and he was eventually sent home in late 1942 and died in early 1943.

General der Artillerie Christian Hansen (1885–1972), commander of X AK since October 1939. Hansen was commissioned as an artillery officer in 1903 and later received General Staff training. During World War I, Hansen served primarily as a high-level staff officer on the Western Front. In the post-war Reichswehr, he rose steadily and was given command of 25. Infanterie-Division in 1936. He was still in command of this unit at the start of World War II, but it was assigned a defensive role in the Saar. Hansen's first command experience in combat was leading X AK in the invasion of Holland in 1940, then in *Barbarossa* in 1941. Although he later succeeded Busch in command of AOK 16 in 1943, Hansen's health was poor and he retired for medical reasons in 1944.

SS-Gruppenführer und Generalleutnant der Waffen-SS Theodor Eicke (1892–1943), commander of the SS-Division 'Totenkopf' since November 1939. A high school dropout who had difficulty holding a civilian job and became involved in the political violence sweeping across Germany in the 1920s, Eicke found a home in the SS. Although Eicke had served only as an enlisted man in the Bavarian Army in World War I, he rose quickly into leadership positions in the SS because of his ardent Nazi political attitudes and blind obedience to orders. He proved a brutal and efficient commander at Dachau concentration camp in 1933–34 and was directly involved in the murder of SA leaders in the 'Night of the Long Knives'. As inspector of concentration camps during 1934–39, Eicke played a key role in implementing Hitler's 'New Order'. When the decision was made to form Waffen-SS divisions at the start of the war, Eicke was selected to form 'Totenkopf' division from his camp guards. Despite the fact that Eicke had only limited military and civilian education and no experience leading troops in combat, the Third Reich entrusted one of its best-equipped divisions to him. Under his command, the division gained a reputation for battlefield atrocities and brutality, as well as unnecessarily heavy casualties. Eicke was badly wounded when his vehicle hit a mine two weeks after the beginning of *Barbarossa* and thus missed the battle of Staraya Russa. By the time he returned to 'Totenkopf' on 21 September 1941, the German offensive was coming to a close. His only son, Hermann Eicke, was serving as a junior enlisted man in 'Totenkopf' and was killed on 2 December, a month before the Demyansk–Kholm campaign started. After Demyansk, Eicke was killed in 1943 when his Fieseler Storch was shot down near Kharkov during Manstein's 'Backhand Blow' counteroffensive. Eicke was a thug with no real military skill and his only redeeming grace in the eyes of his superiors was his willingness to obey any order, no matter how criminal.

General der Artillerie Walther von Seydlitz-Kurzbach (1888–1976), commander of 12. Infanterie-Division and then Gruppe Seydlitz, was responsible for leading the offensive to restore communications with the Demyansk pocket. Seydlitz came from an impeccable Prussian military family and he was commissioned as an artillery officer in 1908. During World War I, he served on both the Eastern and Western Fronts. He was given command of 12. Infanterie-Division in March 1940 and after Demyansk, he was rewarded with the Oak Leaves to his Ritterkreuz der Eisernes Kreuz and command of LI AK in AOK 6. When his corps was surrounded at Stalingrad, Seydlitz recognized that AOK 6's only hope was to mount a breakout attempt, but Paulus ignored him. When AOK 6 finally surrendered, Seydlitz became an active collaborator in Soviet captivity and leader of the Anti-Nazi League of German Officers. For this treason, Hitler sentenced him to death *in absentia*. Despite his cooperation, after the war the Soviets no longer found him useful and sentenced him for war crimes, for which he served five years in prison.

Generalmajor Theodor Scherer (1889–1951), commander of 281. Sicherungs-Division and the disparate collection of units comprising

SS-Gruppenführer Theodor Eicke played a critical role during the first six months of the Demyansk campaign, with his Kampfgruppe Eicke holding the western end of the pocket and then leading the breakout attack in April 1942. Eicke lacked the professional skill of most of the other German regular army division commanders, but he impressed Hitler with his fanatical defence. (Bundesarchiv, Bild 101III-Wiegand-116-03, Fotograf: Wiegand)

Kampfgruppe Scherer surrounded at Kholm. Scherer was commissioned in the Bavarian Army in 1910 and served in World War I until he was captured by the British during the battle of the Somme in July 1916. Returning to Germany after the war, Scherer left the army and joined the Bavarian police from 1920 to 1935. When Hitler reinstated conscription and began enlarging the army, Scherer rejoined and became an infantry battalion commander in 1935 and an infantry regiment commander in 1938. He led an infantry regiment during the assault crossing of the Marne River in June 1940. In March 1941, he was put in charge of security at the Führer's headquarters. When Soviet rear-area partisans began to harass Heeresgruppe Nord's lines of communications, Scherer was given command of 281. Sicherungs-Division and tasked with neutralizing the threat. For his epic defence of the Kholm pocket for 105 days, he was awarded the Ritterkreuz mit Eichenlauband and command of 83. Infanterie-Division. However shortly after Scherer took command of this unit, the bulk of the division was surrounded at Velikiye Luki in November 1942. Despite Scherer's desperate efforts to rescue his division – he was located outside the pocket – over 7,000 of his men were lost when the town fell in January 1943. As a commander, Scherer was a soldier's soldier, who instilled confidence in his men even under the most extreme conditions.

Oberst Fritz Morzik (1891–1985), *Lufttransportführer* (air transport leader) in charge of the Demyansk airlift. Morzik was an army NCO at the start of World War I who volunteered for training as an aerial observer. After serving in this role on the Western Front in 1914–15, he received pilot training and was sent to Palestine in 1916 with Fliegerabteilung 300. Morzik spent a year flying Rumpler C.Is on reconnaissance and bombing missions against the British. Returning to Germany, Morzik was retrained as a fighter pilot and flew first with Jasta 26 (at the same time as Hermann Göring) in 1917, then served on home defence duties in 1918. He left the service after the war and worked as a test pilot for Junkers and as a commercial flight instructor. Later, Morzik established his reputation as an exceptional pilot by winning first place in the 1929 and 1930 International Tourist Plane Contests, which also helped to enhance Germany's prestige in the aviation field. When the Luftwaffe was formed, Morzik served in pilot training roles. At the start of World War II, he was put in command of the Luftwaffe's transport units and helped plan the airborne operations in the 1940–41 campaigns. Morzik's skill at improvisation under pressure was a key factor in the success of the Demyansk and Kholm airlifts. He also frequently exceeded his authority in order to accomplish his mission and used his contacts at the Ministry of Aviation (RLM) and Junkers to gather resources that were not immediately available through normal channels.

SOVIET

General-Colonel Pavel A. Kurochkin (1900–1989), commander of the North-western Front from August 1941 to November 1942, then commander of 11th Army from November 1942 to March 1943. Kurochkin joined the Red Army in 1918 and served as a cavalry officer in the Russian Civil War. Between the wars, he received a thorough military education at the Frunze Military Academy and in the General Staff Academy. By 1935, Kurochkin was in command of a cavalry division and a peer of Georgy Zhukov. Kurochkin was probably aided by his cavalry connections in surviving Stalin's purges of 1937–40 and emerged as one of the few remaining professionally trained division commanders. He commanded a rifle corps in the Russo-Finnish War and served on the Mongolian border in 1940. During the early stages of the German invasion, he briefly commanded 20th Army during the battle of Smolensk in July 1941 and then 43rd Army in August. During the Demyansk campaign, he did the best he could with grossly insufficient forces and proved himself willing to gamble with high-risk tactics. After his failure to crush the Demyansk pocket, the Stavka demoted Kurochkin to command 11th Army but was reinstated in command of the North-western Front in July 1943. He spent the latter half of the war alternating between army and front-level command assignments and went on to a successful post-war career and retired in 1970. Kurochkin was competent but more of an academic, staff officer-type rather than an aggressive front-line commander.

Marshal Semen K. Timoshenko (1895–1970), commander of the North-western Front from November 1942 to March 1943. Timoshenko was the epitome of a cavalry officer and he skilfully climbed the rungs of the Red Army during the inter-war period to attain the position of People's Commissar of Defence in 1940. He was a close associate of Stalin and other influential members of the Red Army's Konarmia (Cavalry army) from the Russian Civil War days, which helped him to survive the purges and rise well past his level of competence. After the initial Soviet military disasters in the Russo-Finnish War, Stalin sent Timoshenko to take command of the forces in Karelia and he succeeded in bludgeoning his way through the Mannerheim line with artillery, which gave him the appearance of success. At the start of the Russo-German War, he was chairman of the Stavka and briefly commanded the Western Front from July to September 1941 where he led a bitter but unsuccessful defence of Smolensk. Afterwards, Timoshenko was given command of the South-western Front in September 1941 and he was in command of the disastrous Soviet offensive at Kharkov in May 1942 that resulted in the loss of over 200,000 troops. He was briefly sent to command the Stalingrad Front in July 1942 before being sent to take command of the North-western Front. After his failure to crush the German forces at Demyansk, Timoshenko was replaced by

General-Colonel Ivan S. Konev in March 1943. Timoshenko was a failure on each occasion he served as front commander and was kicked upstairs to supervise the Stavka for the rest of the war and never held another field command. Timoshenko had a very poor grasp of operational-level planning and he often failed to learn from his mistakes. On the plus side, Stalin considered him loyal and hard working, if not particularly inspired.

General-Lieutenant Vasiliy I. Morozov (1897–1964), commander of 11th Army from June 1941 to November 1942. Morozov had been conscripted into the Tsarist army before joining the Red Army in 1918. After attending the Frunze Military Academy, he spent most of the inter-war period in command of three different rifle divisions and two rifle corps. Based upon his extensive command experience with infantry units, he was a good fit to command a front-line army in the North-western Front and it was in part due to Morozov's leadership that a significant part of 11th Army survived the retreat across Lithuania and Latvia.

General-Major Nikolai E. Berzarin (1904–1945), commander of 34th Army from December 1941 to October 1942. Berzarin joined the Red Army in 1918 and participated in the Russian Civil War, including the suppression of the Kronstadt Mutiny in 1921. He spent much of the inter-war period in Siberia and commanded 32nd Rifle Division in the battle of Lake Khasan against the Japanese in 1938. At the beginning of the German invasion, Berzarin commanded 27th Army in Estonia, which was the second echelon of the North-western Front. Although not a particularly skilled commander, Berzarin managed to remain an army-level commander for the entire duration of the Great Patriotic War. After leading 5th Shock Army into Berlin, he was killed a month later in a post-war car accident.

General-Colonel Maksim A. Purkaev (1894–1953), commander of 3rd Shock Army from December 1941 to August 1942. Purkaev had been a conscript NCO in the Tsarist army who joined the Red Army in 1918 and fought in the Russian Civil War. After training at the Frunze Military Academy, he served primarily as a staff officer in the inter-war period and was also the Soviet military attaché in Berlin in 1940. Later, Purkaev served as Georgy Zhukov's chief of staff in the Kiev Military District, which probably helped his career. At the start of the German invasion, Purkaev was chief of staff of the South-western Front until it was demolished in the Kiev encirclement. When Zhukov was planning the Winter Counteroffensive, he earmarked Purkaev for command of a shock army, even though Purkaev had only modest prior command experience. He was somewhat miscast as a tactical commander and better suited to playing a supporting role. Purkaev was the Soviet tactical commander at Kholm. Zhukov still favoured him despite his failure at Kholm and ensured that he was given the Kalinin Front for Operation *Mars* in 1943. After this notable Soviet military catastrophe, Purkaev was sent to take command of Soviet forces in the Far East for the rest of the war.

General-Colonel Vasiliy I. Kuznetsov (1894–1964), commander 1st Shock Army November 1941 to May 1942. An experienced infantryman, Kuznetsov was one of only seven corps commanders to survive the Stalinist purges of 1937–41. He was an army commander at the start of the German invasion but his 3rd Army was crushed in White Russia and then his second command, 21st Army, was crushed in the Kiev encirclement. Kuznetsov was finally sent to take command of 1st Shock Army in time for the 1941–42 Winter Counteroffensive. Despite failing to stop the German relief of the Demyansk pocket, Kuznetsov enjoyed a successful career afterwards. Vatutin took him with him to the Southwest Front, where he commanded 1st Guards Army on the Don. In 1944 he returned to the northern part of the Eastern Front as deputy commander of the Baltic Front and in 1945 commanded the 3rd Shock Army that spearheaded the assault that captured the Reichstag.

OPPOSING FORCES

GERMAN

Most of the German units in AOK 16's II and X AK had been on the defensive since October 1941 and consequently, they had time to construct adequate company- and battalion-sized *Stützpunkte* (strongpoints) before the Soviet North-western Front offensive began in January 1942. However, AOK 16 lacked the manpower to form a continuous front and only screening forces covered some sectors. Throughout most of the Demyansk–Kholm campaign, the Germans had minimal armour support and often had to rely upon their artillery or the Luftwaffe to stop Soviet attacks or retake ground. Furthermore, AOK 16 was very low on the OKH's priority list for replacements and supplies, so German units in the campaign could not conduct their preferred style of high-intensity manoeuvre operations. German troops surrounded at Demyansk and Kholm were forced to fight in hastily thrown-together *Kampfgruppen* that included large numbers of non-combat personnel from construction units, police, signal detachments, Luftwaffe ground crew and even veterinary staff.

The formations in AOK 16's II and X AK had suffered over 42,000 casualties since the start of Operation *Barbarossa* and losses were particularly significant in the infantry. AOK 16 had received thousands of replacements, but primarily enlisted men. Most infantry battalions still had 350–500 troops out of their nominal strength of 784 and about three-quarters of their crew-served weapons. German pre-war defensive doctrine stipulated that a

A German sentry scans the shores of Lake Il'men from a well-constructed MG-34 position at Stützpunkt Vzvad in December 1941. Unlike Heeresgruppe Mitte retreating from Moscow, Heeresgruppe Nord had the time to build proper field fortifications that enabled key positions to repulse countless Soviet infantry attacks. Also note that the sentry is equipped with a winter parka. (Ian Barter)

full-strength infantry division could effectively defend a 4–6-mile-wide (6–10km) sector and a regiment could hold a 2-mile-wide (3km) sector. Yet in the AOK 16 area of operations, divisions with 45–60 per cent of their infantry were expected to hold sectors that were 12–15 miles wide (20–25km) and sometimes more. Half-strength infantry regiments were assigned sectors that doctrine stated required a division to hold. Consequently, AOK 16's *Hauptkampflinie* (HKL, main line of resistance) was quite porous and there were negligible tactical reserves available to deal with enemy penetrations. Nevertheless, AOK 16 had not been forced to retreat as other German armies in Russia already had and the morale of its troops was intact. Furthermore, Heeresgruppe Nord's quartermasters had begun to issue winter clothing in October 1941 and enough had reached the AOK 16's front-line troops to keep frostbite casualties to a tolerable level.

Heeresgruppe Nord's primary mobile reserve during the Demyansk–Kholm campaign was Panzer-Regiment 203, an independent Panzer unit formed in France in 1941 and then sent to the Eastern Front during the crisis of December 1941. I/Panzer-Regiment 203 supported X AK until it was transferred back to Germany on 13 January 1943. The other major armoured reserve was provided by the assault guns from Sturmgeschütz-Abteilung 184, which fought at Kholm and in the Ramushevo corridor. 8. Panzer-Division also provided an armoured *Kampfgruppe* to AOK 16 for much of 1942, until the division was transferred to Heeresgruppe Mitte in December 1942.

Unlike Heeresgruppe Mitte, which lost a great deal of its artillery in the retreat from Moscow, AOK 16 still had most of its artillery. All told, II and X AK started the Demyansk–Kholm campaign with over 320 artillery pieces, primarily the division-level 10.5cm l.FH 18 and 15cm s.FH 18 howitzers, but also a battalion of long-range 10cm s.K 18 cannons and a battalion of 21cm Mörsers. The infantry divisions had the bulk of their 75mm and 15cm infantry guns to provide regimental-level fires. Although AOK 16 held a considerable advantage over the North-western Front in terms of the quality and quantity of its artillery, the entire Wehrmacht was experiencing shortages of 10.5cm and 15cm artillery ammunition in the winter of 1941–42 because of Hitler's failure to put German industry on a wartime footing. AOK 16 had begun the Demyansk–Kholm campaign with about three days worth of ammunition for its divisional artillery, which was quickly exhausted in the early stages of the Soviet counteroffensive. Inside the Demyansk pocket, Brockdorff-Ahlefeldt's artillery was limited to firing only in dire emergencies until a land resupply route was reopened.

However, the most critical deficiency in AOK 16's defences – aside from shortage of manpower – was its anti-tank capabilities, since the German *Panzerjäger* were still dependent upon the inadequate PaK 36 37mm gun. Typically, each division had only three or four PaK 38 50mm anti-tank guns, supplemented with six or seven Russian 45mm guns. Nor were the handful of short-barrelled PzKpfw III tanks and StuG III assault guns able to defeat Soviet T-34 or KV-1 tanks, despite their rarity on this front. Instead, the German *Stützpunkte* relied upon Teller anti-tank mines and obstacles to keep the occasional Soviet medium tanks out of the fortified towns.

X Armeekorps

At the beginning of January 1942, X AK defended the north-central sector from Lake Il'men down to Demyansk with three divisions – 30. and 290. Infanterie-Division and SS-Division 'Totenkopf' – deployed along a 55-mile-long (90km) front. Hansen had the bulk of his combat power deployed in the centre and right of his sector, focused on holding the towns of Lychkovo and Luzhno. The SS-'Totenkopf' had gone into Russia with 17,265 men in June 1941 and had suffered 9,724 casualties by 5 January 1942, but still fielded six infantry battalions, a motorcycle battalion and four artillery battalions. The 30. Infanterie-Division holding Lychkovo was reinforced with Infanterie-Regiment 368 from Scherer's 281. Sicherungs-Division, giving the division a total of 11 infantry battalions. Oddly, Hansen assigned 290. Infanterie-Division to hold a 28-mile (45km) sector on the corps' left flank with only eight infantry battalions. That division's three infantry regiments held an 18-mile-long (30km) sector between Tulitovo and Vershin, but the last 10 miles (16km) to Lake Il'men – which ran through the marshy estuaries of the Lovat and Pola rivers – was covered only by a thin screen of patrols and Panzerjäger-Abteilung 290 dug in at the fishing village of Vzvad. Hansen had just received the battered 18. Infanterie-Division (mot.), transferred from AOK 18 after the defeat at Tikhvin, which he placed behind Staraya Russa as AOK 16's reserve force. This motorized division only had one-third of its personnel and vehicles left, comprising just five infantry companies in a single reduced-strength regiment. Hansen had the equivalent of 27 infantry battalions and 15 artillery battalions. Owing to the static nature of operations on this front, the German units still had most of their horses; for example, 290. Infanterie-Division had over 5,000 horses, of which 1,500 were local replacement horses. However, fuel for the remaining vehicles was in short supply.

Soviet infantry reinforcements moving up to the front, January 1942. The North-western Front counteroffensive was hindered by lack of adequate roads or railways for its lines of communication. Reinforcements were forced to detrain over 60 miles (95km) from the front and walk for days across frozen lakes and marshes to reach the front. As evident in this photo, few trucks were available. (RIA Novosti, 893880)

Throughout most of 1942, SS-'Totenkopf' Division provided the backbone of the German defence inside the Demyansk pocket. Although the Waffen-SS troops had earned a reputation for tenacity (and atrocities), SS-'Totenkopf' had suffered more casualties than any other division in Heeresgruppe Nord and many German army officers held a negative opinion of Eicke's military skills. It did not help that Eicke claimed that his division was being bled white at Demyansk and went over Busch's head directly to Himmler with requests to relieve 'Totenkopf', while in fact army units such as 5. and 8. Jäger-Divisionen suffered a far higher casualty rate during the Demyansk Campaign.

II Armeekorps

The II AK defended a 60-mile-long (100km) sector from east of Luzhno down to Lake Seliger with three divisions – 12., 32. and 123. Infanterie-Divisionen. Like Hansen, Brockdorff-Ahlefeldt kept the bulk of his combat power in the centre of his sector while using covering forces to screen his extended right flank. The II AK had not been as heavily involved in the fighting in the autumn of 1941 as X AK and had suffered 22 per cent fewer casualties. Consequently, Brockdorff-Ahlefeldt's units were in better shape and 12. Infanterie-Division was near full strength. All told, II AK comprised 33 infantry battalions and 13 artillery battalions in January 1942.

On the extreme right of II AK, 123. Infanterie-Division held a 45-mile-wide (70km) sector between Lake Vel'yo and Ostashkov, but it was too spread out to form a main line of resistance and instead focused on blocking positions. The 123. Infanterie-Division had suffered 34 per cent casualties since the start of Operation Barbarossa, including 1,229 dead. Recognizing the vulnerability of the thinly manned II AK sector, the OKH transferred two infantry regiments from France in December 1941 and they arrived just before the Soviet Winter Counteroffensive began. Infanterie-Regiment 189 from 81. Infanterie-Division detrained at Toropets on 5 January and Infanterie-Regiment 376 from 225. Infanterie-Division was attached to 12. Infanterie-Division. Both formations were at full strength but totally unprepared to operate in sub-zero conditions.

Luftwaffe

Luftflotte I provided air support to Heeresgruppe Nord and had to divide its available resources between the siege of Leningrad, containing Soviet attacks on the Volkhov front and sustaining the Demyansk and Kholm pockets. After six months of continuous operations, the Luftwaffe was reduced to near combat ineffectiveness by late December 1941 and many units were withdrawn to Germany to refit. At the beginning of January 1942, Fliegerkorps I provided direct support to AOK 16 with a dozen Bf-109F fighters flying from the airfield at Staraya Russa and about 60 He-111 and Ju-88 bombers based at Dno with II/KG-4 and I/KG-3. Despite its weakened state, Fliegerkorps I still held air superiority over Demyansk at the start of the Soviet counteroffensive, but this was directly challenged by the VVS in February 1942. In preparation for the German relief operations, Fliegerkorps I was reinforced with 30 Bf-109F fighters from III/JG-3 and 30 Ju-87D dive-bombers from III/StG 1.

Once it became necessary to provide daily aerial resupply missions to the encircled garrisons at Demyansk and Kholm, Fliegerkorps I was able to organize quickly a resupply operation with the forces at hand. Although the Luftwaffe had gained experience with large-scale air transport operations over Crete in May 1941, those efforts were short in duration and intended only to supply 30,000 light infantry. Supplying an army of 96,000 troops with artillery for a period of months had never been attempted by any air force before. However, the Luftwaffe benefited from the fact that the well-equipped air base at Dno was close enough to Demyansk to support a decent sortie rate and Soviet aerial resistance was initially uncoordinated. As the air resupply operation began, the Oberkommando der Luftwaffe (OKL) made the decision to form ad hoc transport units from aviation training schools in Germany and sent them to reinforce Morzik's resupply operation. Although the Ju-52 tri-motor formed the backbone of the operation, a number of Ju-86, Ju-90 and Fw-200 transports were also sent. In addition to daily delivery of supplies, the airlift operation also brought in a significant number of reinforcements and evacuated casualties, which helped to sustain morale in the Demyansk pocket.

In early 1942 the Luftwaffe began forming its first ground combat division from surplus personnel in order to assist the hard-pressed army in Russia. Luftwaffe-Division Meindl was formed on 26 February 1942 under Generalmajor Eugen Meindl and assigned to AOK 16. Although composed of six field regiments, Division Meindl had no artillery and was originally conceived as security troops rather than front-line infantry. Instead, the division was committed as individual battalions as it arrived and several were flown directly into the Demyansk pocket to provide replacements.

SOVIET

The North-western Front suffered 87,000 casualties and was forced to retreat over 350 miles (560km) in the first 18 days of Operation *Barbarossa*. Most of the tanks and heavy artillery belonging to the front were lost in the headlong retreat across Lithuania and Latvia. Although the Stavka was able to raise dozens of new rifle divisions during the summer of 1941, most went to reinforce the Western Front in front of Moscow and 34th Army was the only significant reinforcement Kurochkin received during that summer. Between the battle of Soltsy in July 1941 and the end of the year, the North-

western Front suffered another 178,000 casualties, leaving Kurochkin with nine burnt-out rifle divisions between the 11th and 34th Armies, limited artillery and a handful of tanks. Morozov's 11th Army had about 35,000 troops in five badly mauled divisions, each with no more than 4,000–6,000 troops. The 180th and 182nd Rifle Divisions were odd units that had been incorporated whole from the Estonian Army in September 1940 and still retained non-Soviet equipment. Morozov had very limited artillery but he received about 90 tanks before the counteroffensive, including 15 KV heavy tanks and 30 T-34s. Berzarin's 34th Army was a mixed bag of about 30,000 troops in five depleted rifle divisions, no army-level artillery and only a single battalion of tanks. Throughout much of the Winter Counteroffensive, Berzarin's forces were incapable of much beyond fixing attacks.

Most of the Red Army infantry units in 11th and 34th Armies had been roughly handled in the summer fighting of 1941. According to the 6 December *Shtat* (table of organization), a Soviet rifle division was authorized a strength of 11,907 men and 36 artillery pieces, but many rifle units in the North-western Front were at 50 per cent strength or less. The 180th and 23rd Rifle Divisions were typical, with 5,250 and 6,626 men. In 180th Rifle Division, its three infantry regiments had 1,200–1,450 men each, or 40–48 per cent of their nominal strength. Each regiment had nine rifle companies with about 80 men each, three machine-gun companies, a mortar company with several 82mm mortars, an anti-tank battery and some pioneers. Aside from a single 50-man SMG company armed with PPsh sub-machine guns, infantry firepower was limited since most troops still used the 7.62mm Mosin-Nagant M1891/30 bolt-action rifles. Rifle units were particularly hampered by insufficient automatic weapons firepower, with an average of only four DP light machine guns instead of nine in each company and six heavy machine guns in each regiment instead of 12. Nor could the DP light machine gun overpower the German MG-38 in a firefight, owing to low cyclic rate and lack of belt feed. Furthermore, morale was low in many battered Soviet rifle units and significant numbers of troops were deserting to the Germans on a daily basis.

It was not until the fall of Kalinin on 16 December that the Stavka considered sending any significant reinforcements to Kurochkin. At that point, the Stavka decided to redesignate 60th Army, forming around Moscow, as 3rd Shock Army and 27th Army as 4th Shock Army. Both formations would lead the southern pincer of the North-western Front's Winter Counteroffensive, although they would switch back and forth between the

Northwest and Kalinin fronts. Purkaev's 3rd Shock Army totaled 51,500 troops in three rifle divisions, six rifle brigades and six ski battalions. All three rifle divisions were experienced but rebuilt formations with no more than 6,000–10,000 troops. The rifle brigades were new units, formed from training schools, with no combat experience. The 3rd Shock Army had 142 artillery pieces, giving it the most firepower of any formation in Kurochkin's command, but far below what was expected of a shock formation. Purkaev had only a single tank battalion with 35 tanks and no cavalry. Eremenko's 4th Shock Army had about 60,000 troops in five rifle divisions, one rifle brigade and two ski battalions; except for 249th Rifle Division formed from NKVD personnel, all these units were newly raised formations with no experience.

Soviet pre-war deep battle doctrine had envisioned conducting encirclement operations with fast-moving full-strength tank and cavalry units in fair weather, not with slow-moving, understrength infantry units in the middle of winter. In preparation for the upcoming second phase of the Soviet Winter Counteroffensive, Zhukov issued instructions to all units to form 'shock groups' in order to break through German fortified positions. The Stavka hastily assembled several shock armies in December 1941 to spearhead front-level offensives, but they lacked any kind of combined arms advantage because they were primarily composed of newly raised infantry formations, with limited artillery and tanks. Engineer capabilities to breach German minefields or wire were virtually non-existent. Consequently, the ability of Soviet shock groups to reduce German *Stützpunkte* in January 1942 was negligible. Even when Soviet shock groups could penetrate thinly held parts of the German HKL, they had no real ability to conduct doctrinal deep battle because of the lack of cavalry or large tank formations.

Two innovations that the North-western Front relied heavily upon were the new ski battalions and aerosan battalions. The Red Army had been working on developing combat snowmobiles (aerosans) since 1919 and by the autumn of 1941 they had begun to form the first Combat Aerosled Battalions (BASB) and Transport Aerosled Battalions (TASB). Although too lightly built for use in direct combat, the NKL-16 and RF-8-GAZ-98

LEFT
A platoon of white-clad Soviet ski troops emerge from a forest. The 3rd Shock Army organized small but powerful shock groups that quickly pushed in the right flank of AOK 16 and helped create the conditions for the Demyansk pocket. (Courtesy of the Central Museum of the Armed Forces Moscow via Stavka)

RIGHT
German troops from 123. Infanterie-Division man a fighting position overlooking Lake Seliger. The German positions in this sector were too dispersed to stop 3rd Shock Army's assault and could do little more than delay the Soviet steamroller. (Ian Barter)

aerosleds were ideal for moving troops across the ice-covered lakes in the North-western Front sector. Each aerosled was equipped with a small aircraft or truck engine and could approach speeds of 20mph (32km/h) over ice, which gave the Soviets a distinct advantage in mobility in the winter. Further capitalizing on Russian expertise in winter warfare – much of it learned at great cost in the Russo-Finnish War – the Stavka formed a large number of ski battalions in December 1941. The early battalions were formed primarily from Communist youth sports groups with ski experience and fielded about 400 ski infantry and a light mortar battery. While ski battalions and aerosled battalions could not capture German *Stützpunkte*, they were a major surprise to the Germans when they first appeared. The North-western Front received 13 ski battalions and seven aerosan battalions in January–February 1942.

The gravest deficiency for the North-western Front was in field artillery. Divisional fire support assets were very weak in January 1942. The 180th Rifle Division's artillery regiment had a total of 19 artillery pieces instead of 24 and this unit was considered fortunate. Other rifle divisions had, at best, a few batteries of 76.2mm field guns and 120mm mortars, which had limited effect against German defensive fieldworks. The only medium and heavy artillery was concentrated in a few army-level artillery regiments. All told, North-western Front started the counteroffensive with about 100 76mm field guns, 60 medium howitzers and 24 multiple rocket launchers. Stocks of artillery ammunition were very limited, enabling only short bombardments. Furthermore, the ability of Soviet artillery to provide indirect fire in January 1942 was minimal, owing to the limited number of radio or telephone-equipped forward observers. Combat logistics were also a serious problem for the North-western Front. Prior to the start of the counteroffensive, riflemen in the shock groups of 11th Army were issued 100 rounds of ammunition and two hand grenades, which were sufficient for only the first day of the operation. In 3rd Shock Army, the assault troops had not eaten for two days prior to the offensive and were told that they could eat when they captured the German supply depots at Kholm and Toropets. Kurochkin was forced to conduct a major offensive not only with inadequately trained and equipped forces, but insufficient rations even to feed his troops regularly.

Kurochkin depended upon the VVS-North-western Front for air support, but their handful of aviation regiments were in even worse shape than Fliegerkorps I in January 1942. In this sector, the VVS had about 150 operational aircraft, of which 30 were fighters (mostly LaGG-3). Consequently, when the counteroffensive began the VVS-North-western Front was too feeble to prevent the Demyansk or Kholm airlifts.

ORDER OF BATTLE, 1 JANUARY 1942

GERMAN

16. ARMEE (AOK 16)
Generaloberst Ernst Busch
Polizei-Regiment Nord
I./Panzer-Regiment 203

II AK
(General der Infanterie Walter Graf von Brockdorff-Ahlefeldt)
Reinforced Infanterie-Regiment 189 (from 81. Infanterie-Division)
Artillerie-Abteilung 526 (3 batteries, s.FH)
Artillerie-Abteilung 636 (2 batteries, 21cm Mörser)
1 Battery I./Artillerie-Regiment 818 (10cm s.K 18)
12. Infanterie-Division (Oberst Karl Hernekamp)
    Infanterie-Regiment 27, 48, 89
32. Infanterie-Division (Generalleutnant Wilhelm Bohnstedt)
    Infanterie-Regiment 4, 94, 96
123. Infanterie-Division (Generalleutnant Erwin Rauch)
    Infanterie-Regiment 415, 416, 418
Attached: Sicherungs-Regiment 3

X AK
(General der Artillerie Christian Hansen)
I./Artillerie-Regiment 818 (10cm s.K 18)
1./Artillerie-Abteilung 636 (21cm Mörser)
II/Artillerie-Regiment 207
Reinforced Infanterie-Regiment 368 (from 281. Sicherungs-Division)
SS-Division 'Totenkopf' (Obergruppenführer Theodor Eicke)
    SS-'Totenkopf' Infanterie-Regiment 1, 3
30. Infanterie-Division (General der Infanterie Kurt von Tippelskirch)
    Infanterie-Regiment 6, 26, 46
290. Infanterie-Division (Generalleutnant Theodor Freiherr von Wrede)
    Infanterie-Regiment 501, 502, 503
18. Infanterie-Division (mot.) (Oberst Werner von Erdmannsdorff)
    Infanterie-Regiment (mot.) 30, 51

Kampfgruppe Scherer
I, II/IR 386 from 218. Infanterie-Division
I, II/IR 416 from 123. Infanterie-Division
(Gebirgs) Jagdkommando 8
Maschinengewehr-Bataillon 10
Landesschützen-Bataillon 869
53. Reserve-Polizei-Abteilung
65. Reserve-Polizei-Abteilung

Reinforcements:

January:
I, III/Infanterie-Regiment 376

February:
XXXIX AK headquarters (General der Panzertruppen Hans Jürgen von Arnim)
218. Infanterie-Division
Kampfgruppe Crissoli, 8. Panzer-Division
5. leichte Infanterie-Division
8. leichte Infanterie-Division
Luftwaffe-Division Meindl

March:
329. Infanterie-Division
122. Infanterie-Division
Gebirgsjäger-Regiment 206/7. Gebirgs-Division

April:
Freikorps 'Dänemark'

July:
126. Infanterie-Division

January 1943:
58. Infanterie-Division
225. Infanterie-Division
254. Infanterie-Division

SOVIET

NORTH-WESTERN FRONT
General-Colonel Kurochkin
    Chief of Staff: General-Lieutenant Vatutin
    Total strength: 170,000 troops, 186 tanks

11th Army
Total: 37,022 troops, 133 guns, 85 tanks
    5 Rifle Divisions (84, 180, 182, 188, 254)
    3 Tank Battalions (103, 150, 161)
    10 Ski Battalions

34th Army
Total: 36,000 troops, 105 guns, 22 tanks
    5 Rifle Divisions (26, 163, 202, 241, 245)
    1 Tank Battalion (85)

3rd Shock Army
Total: 51,600 troops, 142 guns
    3 Rifle Divisions (23, 33, 257)
    6 Rifle Brigades (20, 27, 31, 42, 45, 54)
    6 Ski Battalions
    1 Tank Battalion (170)

4th Shock Army
Total: 70,500 troops, 31 tanks
    5 Rifle Divisions (249, 332, 334, 358, 360)
    3 Rifle Brigades (21, 39, 51)
    7 Ski Battalions
    270th Gun Artillery Regiment
    109th Guards Mortar Battalion
    1 Tank Battalion (171)

Reinforcements:

February 1942:
1st Guards Rifle Corps
    7th Guards Rifle Division
    3 Rifle Brigades (14, 15, 52)
    74th Naval Rifle Brigade
    69th Tank Brigade
    3 Ski Battalions

2nd Guards Rifle Corps (General-Major Aleksandr I. Liziukov)
    8th Guards Rifle Division
    3 Rifle Brigades (26, 27, 38)
    75th Naval Rifle Brigade
    3 Ski Battalions

1st Shock Army (General-Lieutenant V. I. Kuznetsov)
    6 Rifle Brigades (2nd Guards; 41, 44, 46, 47, 50)
    1 Naval Rifle Brigade (62)
    10 Ski Battalions

From Kalinin Front: 1 rifle division (130) and 1 rifle brigade (86) and 1 naval rifle brigade (154)

March 1942:
1st and 2nd Manoeuvre Airborne Brigades
204th Airborne Brigade

April 1942:
53rd Army (General-Major A. S. Ksenofontov)
    4 Rifle Divisions (166, 235, 241, 250)

May 1942:
27th Army (General-Major F. P. Oserov)
    1 Rifle Division (384)

OPPOSING PLANS

GERMAN

By the beginning of January 1942, the Germans were hard pressed almost everywhere along the length of the Eastern Front and Heeresgruppe Mitte – with the largest share of German combat power – had suffered a major defeat at Moscow. A number of senior German commanders, including Leeb in Heeresgruppe Nord, were on the verge of nervous collapse after six months of intense combat. The OKH ordered Leeb to besiege Leningrad with the bulk of AOK 18, while AOK 16 protected the army group's right flank. Both Leeb and Busch would be satisfied if AOK 16 merely held its ground with the minimum forces necessary until Germany could regain the initiative. Both commanders also recommended pulling the bulk of II and X AK back closer to the Lovat River to shorten their lines, but since neither corps came under serious attack in December, Hitler forbade it. Hitler's refusal to abandon territory, no matter how devoid of strategic value, was a critical factor in shaping the Demyansk campaign for the next year.

Soviet infantry assault a German-held village. Most of the North-western Front attacks in January–February 1942 were infantry heavy with very little armour or artillery support. Consequently, Soviet shock groups had great difficulty capturing any German position protected by barbed wire, mines and interlocking fields of fire from automatic weapons. (Courtesy of the Central Museum of the Armed Forces Moscow via Stavka)

Since he could not withdraw his exposed forces, Busch ordered II and X AK to construct a robust line of *Stützpunkte*, particularly in the centre around Demyansk. However, he took great risk on both flanks, assigning 123. and 290. Infanterie-Divisionen to hold ridiculously long sectors and with no real tactical reserves to support them. The main goal was to hold the railheads at Staraya Russa and Toropets, which the Wehrmacht needed to sustain its front-line units, but Busch regarded minor losses of marshland and forests as an acceptable risk. Busch was able to persuade Leeb to transfer the battered 18. Infanterie-Division (mot.) to Staraya Russa just before the Soviet counteroffensive began – a move that probably saved AOK 16 from utter defeat – and Leeb was able to convince the OKH that the risk to the boundary with Heeresgruppe Mitte required reinforcements. The OKH began transferring divisions from France in response to the Moscow counteroffensive and Leeb was promised two more divisions. Thus, German planning in AOK 16 at the beginning of the year rested upon the need to hold on until new forces arrived to plug the gaps in its lines.

SOVIET

Oddly, the Soviets did not set out to encircle II AK at Demyansk. The North-western Front had been a backwater sector since September 1941 and it was only German defeats on neighbouring sectors that caused the Stavka to reconsider another offensive on the Staraya Russa axis. Heeresgruppe Nord's defeat at Tikhvin on 8 December and Heeresgruppe Mitte's loss of Kalinin on 16 December had seriously weakened the German position in northern Russia. Stalin, convinced that the Wehrmacht was near collapse on all fronts, directed the Stavka to prepare a second phase of Winter Counteroffensive operations to begin in early January 1942. He directed that the newly created Volkhov Front would breach AOK 16's defences north of Novgorod, then advance eastwards to raise the siege of Leningrad. Simultaneously, the Kalinin Front would attack towards Rzhev and then in conjunction with the Western Front, towards Vyazma. Logically, the North-western Front was in a good position to support both major axes of advance by its neighbours, by attacking the boundary between Heeresgruppe Nord and Heeresgruppe Mitte. An attack by North-western Front, even if only partially successful, could help to tie down German reserves and help its neighbouring fronts to achieve decisive results.

The Stavka issued Directive No. 005868 for the Demyansk–Kholm operation to General-Colonel Pavel A. Kurochkin's North-western Front on 18 December 1941. His chief of staff was General-Lieutenant Nikolai F. Vatutin, one of the most talented senior officers in the Red Army and the man who planned the previous counterattacks at Soltsy and Staraya Russa. At the start, neither Demyansk nor Kholm was specified as an important objective and the encirclement of large German forces was not expected. Rather, the Stavka expected the North-western Front to attack with six division-sized shock groups no later than 26 December in order to punch a hole through AOK 16's thin lines south of Lake Il'men, liberate Staraya Russa and then push exploitation forces 95 miles (150km) west to Dno to sever German lines of communications. Kurochkin was also expected to pivot his shock groups north-west from Staraya Russa, to assist the Volkhov Front in destroying German forces at Novgorod. Furthermore, Kurochkin would receive 3th and 4th Shock Armies from Stavka Reserves and use them to tear apart the boundary between Heeresgruppe Nord and Heeresgruppe Mitte and push on to seize the German supply base at Toropets, thereby supplementing the Kalinin Front's offensive against AOK 9 at Rzhev. Thus, rather than a converging encirclement operation, the North-western Front's two pincers were actually intended to diverge.

Despite these grand objectives, the Stavka provided neither the time nor resources to conduct a protracted offensive, which forced Kurochkin to fight a stone soup type of battle, stopping every time his resources were depleted and asking for more reinforcements and supplies. Since no significant cavalry or tank units were transferred from Stavka Reserve, the requirement to conduct a deep exploitation as far as Dno was absurd. Owing to widespread difficulties in moving troops to the front, Marshal Boris Shaposhnikov, chief of the Red Army's General Staff, was able to convince Stalin to delay the counteroffensive until 30 December. Even with this delay, the transfer of 3rd Shock Army from Moscow took much longer than expected owing to shortages of fuel, trucks and available trains. Contrary to many German accounts, the atrocious winter weather also greatly affected Soviet units formed from hastily mobilized raw recruits, who were no more accustomed to living outdoors in sub-zero temperatures than the Germans. Furthermore, Kurochkin was being asked to conduct a major counteroffensive in an area with few roads, no significant numerical superiority and grossly insufficient logistics. At this point in the war, Soviet industry was still suffering from relocation to the Urals, meaning that new tanks, artillery ammunition and other supplies were not available in quantity yet and Stalin's penchant for attacking everywhere was spreading the available resources very thinly. Kurochkin was instructed to make do and rely upon the capture of German supply dumps at Staraya Russa and Toropets to sustain his offensive momentum.

A typical German *Stutzpünkt* in the winter of 1941–42. In addition to trenches and barbed wire, the Germans usually dug out cellars within the peasant *izbas* (huts) and lined them with logs or sandbags to provide a refuge from Soviet artillery fire. The only way for the Soviets usually to take these positions was to set the buildings afire with Katyusha rockets or incendiary shells. (Nik Cornish at Stavka)

Despite their misgivings about success, Kurochkin and Vatutin did the best they could with the resources at hand. Given the force limitations, their objective was not to encircle a large part of AOK 16 – they assumed that the Germans would withdraw most forces behind the Lovat River when their flanks were threatened – but to achieve a deep penetration in the Staraya Russa sector and near Lake Seliger. The pre-war Soviet deep battle (*glubokiy boy*) doctrine emphasized using one or more shock armies (*udarnaia armiia*), supported by heavy artillery, tanks and aircraft, to achieve penetrations of up to 10–15 miles (15–25km) into the depth of the enemy defences in order to enable cavalry and mechanized exploitation forces to get into the enemy rear and sever their lines of communication. However, Kurochkin clearly could not implement this doctrine as intended. Instead, Kurochkin and Vatutin decided to take advantage of the German tendency to use lakes to cover gaps in their continuous front. During the summer months, the numerous lakes in the region had assisted the Germans in conducting an economy of force operation but, once they froze in the winter, the lakes became areas of vulnerability. AOK 16 sent only occasional patrols over Lake Il'men and Lake Seliger and lacked the troops to build effective defences along their shores. Thus Kurochkin and Vatutin decided to play the only advantage they had by using aerosans and ski troops to bypass as much of X AK *Stützpunkt* as possible and seize Staraya Russa with a *coup de main* over the ice. The 11th Army would begin the counteroffensive on 7 January but 3rd and 4th Shock Armies were still not ready and could not join the attack until 9 January.

Kurochkin had another possible trump card – partisans. Many Soviet troops had been cut off during the 1941 Campaign and they had combined with local civilians to form several large partisan units in forests and marshes in the AOK 16 rear areas. Vatutin was able to contact 2nd Partisan Brigade operating near Kholm and it was directed to seize the town just before 3rd Shock Army vanguard arrived. Soviet plans were overly ambitious but neither Kurochkin nor Vatutin had any choice; Stalin had already relieved the last commander of the North-western Front and executed his chief of staff.

THE DEMYANSK CAMPAIGN

THE SOVIET WINTER COUNTEROFFENSIVE, JANUARY 1942

11th Army attacks, 7–30 January

The trouble began on the German left flank, in the marshy delta of the rivers Lovat and Vergot, on the southern edge of Lake Il'men. During the late summer and autumn of 1941, this area was a roadless, mosquito-infested cesspool that the Germans could safely ignore since no Soviet attacks could threaten their supply base at Staraya Russa from this direction. Yet as autumn turned to winter and the marshes began to freeze, Hansen knew that he would have to provide some security measures in this sector so he ordered the fortification of the fishing village at Vzvad near the mouth of the river Lovat and a string of small observation posts built along the west bank of the river to detect any Soviet movements in this area. He also ordered pioneers to emplace mine barriers at likely crossing sites. The right end of this screening line was anchored on a battalion-sized *Stützpunkt* of 290. Infanterie-Division at the village of Tulitovo on the river Lovat. Although this screen line was

A company of Soviet T-60 light tanks moving up the front in early 1942. Although the North-western Front began its counteroffensive with several tank battalions, most of its armour was composed of light T-60s, armed with a 20mm cannon. The T-60 was better suited to the marshy and icy conditions south of Lake Il'men than either the T-34 or KV-1, but it was too lightly armed and protected to assault German *Stützpunkte*. (Courtesy of the Central Museum of the Armed Forces Moscow via Stavka)

Initial phase of North-western Front counteroffensive, 7–31 January 1942

1. 6–7 January, 11th Army begins counteroffensive against left flank of X AK.
2. 7 January, 2nd Shock Army attacks left flank of AOK 16 on Volkhov Front.
3. 9 January, 3rd and 4th Shock Armies begin counteroffensive against right flank of II AK.
4. Routed 123. Infanterie-Division splits, with KG Rauch heading towards Demyansk, KG Stengel heading to Kholm.
5. 3rd Shock Army splits into three parts, heading towards Demyansk, Kholm and Velikiye Luki.
6. German 12. Infanterie-Division sends a *Kampfgruppe* to reinforce the crumbling southern flank.
7. 11 January, 34th Army achieves breakthrough near Pola.
8. 11 January, 39th Army encircles German XXIII AK at Olenino.
9. 12 January, 11th Army invests Staraya Russa and severs road to Demyansk.
10. 15 January, 4th Shock Army destroys IR 189 and captures Andreapol.
11. 19 January, German LIX AK begins arriving at Velikiye Luki.
12. 20 January, 4th Shock Army captures Toropets.
13. 21 January, Kampfgruppe Scherer surrounded at Kholm.
14. 22 January, X AK deploys its limited reserves to prevent encirclement of Staraya Russa.
15. 29 January, 1st GRC arrives inserted into breach east of Staraya Russa.

German infantry man a snow bunker. German troops were able to build effective bunkers from blocks of snow, made harder by pouring water over them, then topped either with timber or rails for overhead protection. These types of field positions were difficult to spot and provided good cover. Note that these German troops are well equipped with winter clothing. (Ian Barter)

thinly manned, Hansen was not particularly worried because he did not believe that the Soviets could move substantial forces across the lake once it froze and even if they could, the Luftwaffe would detect them and destroy them. The rest of 290. Infanterie-Division was deployed in a string of strongpoints stretching from Tulitovo in the west to Pustyn'ka in the east, intended to protect the railway line through Parfino and Pola.

Kurochkin was not deterred by the difficulty of the terrain on the south side of Lake Il'men and directed Morozov to begin moving two strong shock groups, based upon 180th and 188th Rifle Divisions, into the forests on the east bank of the river Vergot in early January. Hidden among the snow-covered silver birch, the shock troops waited, without any fires or shelter for warmth. Meanwhile, Soviet ski troops conducted route reconnaissance missions to identify the areas of best mobility through the 30in.-deep (80cm) snow and to mark them, while pioneers helped to build ice roads for trucks and tanks. Although there were absolutely no roads in this area – which made Hansen confident that no serious attack could come from this direction – Kurochkin and Morozov were able to prepare a narrow mobility corridor through the frozen wilderness. Since the ice over Lake Il'men was now thick enough to support tanks, Morozov brought some of his armour across at night, to avoid detection by the Luftwaffe.

At 2120hrs on the night of 7 January, Hochstand 5 – a German observation post 2 miles (3km) south-east of Stützpunkt Vzvad – reported that enemy ski troops were across the Lovat River. Four hours later, another German outpost reported hearing the sounds of mines detonating near the mouth of the river Red'ya, a tributary of the Lovat. Without any sort of artillery preparation, Morozov moved a reinforced shock group based on 180th Rifle Division across the river Vergot then the Lovat River, to advance south-west down the Red'ya Valley. The Red'ya Valley was 5 miles (8km) long and little more than a ski trail, but it now became 11th Army's main axis of advance. Another regimental-sized shock group headed towards Vzvad, to isolate the German strongpoint. Morozov's choice of an infiltration attack down the Red'ya River valley when the thermometer stood at 17° F (-8° C) caught Hansen completely by surprise and during the night over 4,000 Soviet troops crossed the Lovat, bypassing the ineffectual line of observation posts.

▼ EVENTS

1 Night of 7–8 January 1942: 11th Army conducts a two-division infiltration attack down the Red'ya and Polist river valleys to outflank the main X AK defences east of Tulitovo.

2 8–9 January 1942: the 180th Rifle Division envelops and isolates the German *Stützpunkt* at Tulitovo, which holds out for five weeks.

3 9–10 January 1942: 11th Army overruns or pushes back the German screening forces between the Red'ya and Lovat rivers, opening the approaches to Staraya Russa. The 290. Infanterie-Division pulls in its blocking positions to build a new front on the Lovat.

4 9–10 January 1942: the 84th and 182nd Rifle Divisions advance westwards, cutting the road to Stützpunkt Vzvad and threatening to encircle Staraya Russa from the north.

5 10–11 January 1942: the 188th Rifle Division cuts the road to Demyansk and brings the airstrip under fire.

6 12–13 January 1942: the 382nd Rifle Regiment and three ski battalions advance through a gap in the German defences and envelop the town from the north-west. The Soviet troops fight their way into the south-west corner of Staraya Russa.

7 13 January 1942: A German counterattack destroys the bulk of 382nd Rifle Regiment.

8 17 January 1942: Soviet artillery emplaced north and north-east of Staraya Russa bombards the city with over 2,000 rounds.

9 15–18 January 1942: Hansen moves the Polizei-Regiment Nord and IR 174 from 81. Infanterie-Division to set up blocking positions.

10 24 January 1942: counterattack by IR 174, supported by four PzKpfw IIIs from Panzer-Regiment 203 stops the 84th Rifle Division from advancing further west.

11 30 January 1942. 18: Infanterie-Division (mot.) sends one battalion and its engineers to keep the road to Kholm open.

12 1 February 1942: Gruppe Leopold is cobbled together to hold the river crossing at Davidovo on the Demyansk road.

13 3 February 1942: the lead elements of 1st GRC (14th and 15th Rifle Brigades) try to take the Red'ya River crossing at Davidovo, but they are repulsed.

14 8 February 1942: the 1st GRC arrives at the front and begins pushing toward the Kholm road.

THE BATTLE FOR STARAYA RUSSA, 9 JANUARY TO 8 FEBRUARY 1942

German X AK struggles to prevent overwhelming Soviet forces from cutting off the town.

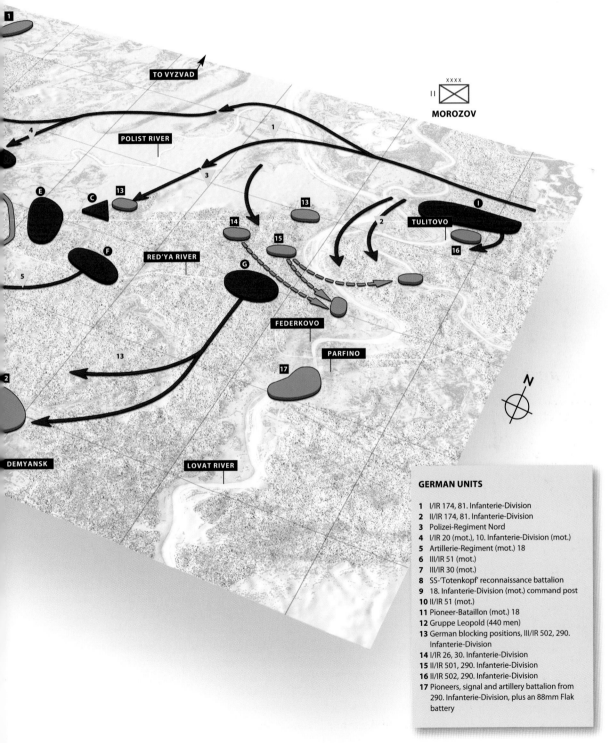

Note: Gridlines are shown at intervals of 5 km/3.10 miles

TO VYZVAD

POLIST RIVER

MOROZOV

RED'YA RIVER

FEDERKOVO

TULITOVO

PARFINO

DEMYANSK

LOVAT RIVER

N

GERMAN UNITS

1 I/IR 174, 81. Infanterie-Division
2 II/IR 174, 81. Infanterie-Division
3 Polizei-Regiment Nord
4 I/IR 20 (mot.), 10. Infanterie-Division (mot.)
5 Artillerie-Regiment (mot.) 18
6 III/IR 51 (mot.)
7 III/IR 30 (mot.)
8 SS-'Totenkopf' reconnaissance battalion
9 18. Infanterie-Division (mot.) command post
10 II/IR 51 (mot.)
11 Pioneer-Bataillon (mot.) 18
12 Gruppe Leopold (440 men)
13 German blocking positions, III/IR 502, 290.
    Infanterie-Division
14 I/IR 26, 30. Infanterie-Division
15 II/IR 501, 290. Infanterie-Division
16 II/IR 502, 290. Infanterie-Division
17 Pioneers, signal and artillery battalion from
    290. Infanterie-Division, plus an 88mm Flak
    battery

German reinforcements from 81. Infanterie-Division checking their equipment in a forest west of Staraya Russa, February 1942. Although the division's IR 386 was detached to delay 3rd Shock Army, the rest of the division was retained to help secure the southern shore of Lake Il'men and assist 18. Infanterie-Division (mot.) in the defence of Staraya Russa. Note the depth of the snow, which was fatiguing for marching infantrymen. (Ian Barter)

Once the sun came up, Luftwaffe reconnaissance quickly confirmed that a large Soviet force was across the Lovat and moving south-west, towards Staraya Russa. By 1000hrs, Hauptmann Günter Pröhl's garrison in Stützpunkt Vzvad was isolated by ski troops, who cut the road to Staraya Russa. Since X AK had very limited reserves, Hansen could only order part of III/IR 502 to move to set up a blocking position at the south end of the Red'ya Valley, while moving two artillery batteries and some engineers into Parfino.

At 2035hrs on 8 January, the Soviet 42nd Rifle Regiment launched a night assault on Stützpunkt Vzvad but was repulsed with heavy losses. Some 120 Soviet troops were captured by Hauptmann Pröhl's men and they revealed details about the unfolding Soviet counteroffensive, which were passed on to Hansen by radio. Hansen ordered Pröhl to hold his position and assured him that the Luftwaffe would provide daily supply drops to his garrison. This marked the beginning of the 13-day siege of Vzvad. The Soviets eventually brought up a few BM-13 multiple rocket launchers and bombarded Stützpunkt Vzvad, setting half the town aflame, but another night attack was repulsed.

Owing to the information from Pröhl, Hansen now knew that he was dealing with a major enemy attack and not raids on isolated outposts. During the night of 8–9 January, he scrambled to try and get more blocking forces to his left flank, but Morozov was several steps ahead of him. Hansen assigned the badly depleted 18. Infanterie-Division (mot.) to defend Staraya Russa but to fill out its ranks he ordered Eicke to send SS-'Totenkopf's reconnaissance battalion there, as well. Hansen sent his only real mobile reserve, Radführer-Abteilung 30, along with a few rifle companies from IR 502 to block the Red'ya Valley. While Hansen was moving up these limited forces, Morozov succeeded in getting some tanks down the Red'ya Valley and conducted a surprise attack against the German company-sized garrison in the village of Yur'evo. The appearance of a few KV-1 tanks at Yur'evo was a great surprise and overwhelmed the German *Panzerjäger* there who were equipped only with anti-tank rifles. With the collapse of his outpost line, Hansen was desperate to establish blocking positions in front of Morozov's shock groups and on the evening of 9 January he ordered II/IR 501 and I/IR 26 – just two battalions – to dig in between the villages of Anuchino and Sloboda. German pioneers also laid a mine barrier with S-mines and Teller mines in front of the villages during the night.

Morozov's ski troops detected the German blocking positions and he began massing his forces for a concerted attack on the morning of 10 January. Soviet probing began at Anuchino around 0935hrs and steadily escalated as tanks and artillery were fed into the battle. Hansen requested Luftwaffe support to break up the Soviet attacks but they were ineffective. At 1450hrs, Morozov launched an attack with one and a half infantry regiments, one pioneer battalion and 30 tanks against Anuchino and Sloboda. Although the attack on Anuchino was repulsed with heavy losses, I/IR 26 at Sloboda lacked effective anti-tank weapons and could not hold; it succeeded in destroying one tank with mines but was bypassed. With his blocking position turned, Hansen was forced to order these blocking units to fall back towards Parfino and the Lovat River, where he had two 88mm flak guns hurriedly brought up to counter Soviet tanks.

Hansen's problems were rapidly escalating as Stützpunkt Vzvad was under continuous pressure and now the Soviet 34th Army was beginning to probe 290. Infanterie-Division's right flank near Stützpunkt Pustyn'ka. Morozov concentrated most of 180th Rifle Division against the German battalion in Stützpunkt Tulitovo, which was gradually encircled, while 188th Rifle Division pushed aggressively down the Red'ya Valley with 14 tanks. Against negligible opposition, 188th Rifle Division reached the outskirts of Staraya Russa and cut the only supply road to II AK at Demyansk on 11 January. Hard on the heels of 188th Rifle Division, 182nd and 84th Rifle Divisions followed down the Red'ya and Polist river valleys, providing Morozov with elements of three divisions outside Staraya Russa by the fourth day of the offensive.

Inside Staraya Russa, Oberst Werner von Erdmannsdorff in command of 18. Infanterie-Division (mot.) hastily deployed his worn-out units to defend the east, northern and western approaches to the city while moving his support units to the south. Erdmannsdorff had 6,500 troops defending a 19-mile (31km) perimeter around Staraya Russa but one-third of them were construction or Luftwaffe personnel. In addition to Erdmannsdorff's five weak battalions, he had the SS-'Totenkopf' reconnaissance battalion hold the vital eastern edge of the city. The garrison inside Staraya Russa did have substantial artillery support, with 28 large-calibre weapons (two 10cm, 13 10.5cm, 14 15cm and two 21cm mortars) and a battery of four 88mm flak guns, but it was very weak in terms of infantry. Nor was the city prepared for all-round defence. Once Morozov brought up more troops, he began to invest Staraya Russa on 12 January. A reinforced shock group from 84th Rifle Division, consisting of 382nd Rifle Division and three ski battalions, made a wide circuit around Staraya Russa and approached the unguarded south-west corner of the city on the morning of 13 January. The sudden appearance of ski troops caught the Germans by surprise and two Soviet battalions severed the main road to Shimsk and the railway line, then advanced into the city. Despite being caught off guard, Erdmannsdorff reacted violently to the Soviet incursion and scraped enough artillerymen and rear area troops together to mount a desperate counterattack. After heavy fighting, both Soviet battalions that had entered the city were destroyed. However, Staraya Russa was still almost entirely encircled and, with the railway line cut, the garrison was dependent upon aerial resupply from Luftflotte I. Compounding the German difficulties, Morozov brought up two artillery groups equipped with 76mm field guns and began to pound the city into rubble. The Germans estimated 2,000–2,500 rounds fell in the city on 17 January alone.

While Erdmannsdorff was hanging on by his fingernails, Hansen was trying to contain the Soviet breakthrough. He moved up the Polizei-Regiment Nord to block the main road west of Staraya Russa, to prevent 11th Army from pushing farther west. As the rest of 81. Infanterie-Division arrived by rail from France, Hansen sent it to reinforce the police and once he had the three battalions of Infanterie-Regiment 174 deployed he planned a counterattack to clear the railway line into Staraya Russa. Reinforced by four PzKpfw III tanks from Panzer-Regiment 203, IR 174 attacked 84th Rifle Division north-west of Staraya Russa on 24 January and was able to regain some ground, but could not re-open the railway line. By the end of January, 11th Army still had a fairly tight ring around Staraya Russa but the city was never completely surrounded. Erdmannsdorff's 18. Infanterie-Division (mot.) suffered over 1,000 casualties since the beginning of the Soviet counteroffensive, but he was still able to scrape up an infantry battalion and some engineers to establish blocking positions along the Kholm road, keeping a tenuous supply line open.

Unable to storm his way into Staraya Russa or completely encircle the city, Morozov settled into siege operations and turned to request additional reinforcements. In response, the Stavka promised to send 1st and 2nd GRC to reinforce the North-western Front, although these units would not arrive until early February. In the meantime, Morozov was eager to show some success and he decided to finish off Stützpunkt Vzvad. Despite repelling repeated Soviet assaults, Hauptmann Pröhl's garrison was near the end of its tether and its ammunition. On 20 January, Busch finally gave Pröhl permission to evacuate Vzvad and Kampfgruppe Pröhl marched 12 miles across the open ice of Lake Il'men in temperatures of -58° F (-50° C) to reach German positions near Staraya Russa. Soviet troops advanced into the burnt wreckage of Vzvad, the only important position to fall to 11th Army in January.

34th Army attacks, January 1942

Kurochkin had not assigned any major offensive tasks to Berzarin's 34th Army since it was the weakest of his subordinate armies. Instead, Berzarin was directed to form two division-sized shock groups to support the efforts of 11th Army and 3rd Shock Army but otherwise, to fix as much of AOK 16 in place as possible with diversionary attacks. Consequently, 34th Army conducted only minor attacks against the German 30., 12. and 32. Infanterie-Divisionen during the first few days of the North-western Front's counteroffensive, and Busch recognized that he could afford to draw upon these divisions for reinforcements to patch up his threatened flanks.

By 10 January, Berzarin saw an opportunity to attack the right flank of 290. Infanterie-Division, which had been weakened as that division stripped troops from its right flank to create a new front on the Lovat facing west. The main defence in the east was based around Stützpunkt Pustyn'ka, with over 150 troops from IR 503 and it was supported by three nearby company-sized strongpoints known as Robinson Crusoe, Devil's Island and Icicle. However, the *Stützpunkt* had only limited ability to provide mutual fire support and could not prevent Soviet ski troops and a regiment from 254th Rifle Division from infiltrating through the marshes and then cutting their supply lines during the night of 10–11 January. The first attack by 254th Rifle Division on Stützpunkt Pustyn'ka was broken up by German artillery fire, but soon all the strongpoints in this sector were surrounded. One by one, 34th Army eliminated these trapped positions and their garrisons. Once 290. Infanterie-

Division's right flank was punched in, Berzarin widened the breach by sending in 202nd Rifle Division, which was able to advance 8 miles (13km) and cut the Parfino–Lychkovo railway line. The 290. Infanterie-Division was forced to refuse its crumbling right flank while it was also refusing its left flank, leaving the division in a long, thin salient between 11th and 34th Armies.

3rd Shock Army attacks, 9–20 January 1942

The right flank of II AK, held by 123. Infanterie-Division, was in an even more parlous state than Hansen's left flank. Generalleutnant Erwin Rauch had the bulk of his division, Infanterie-Regimenter 415 and 418, holding the area between Lake Vel'yo and the north-west corner of Lake Seliger. His defence was based upon a string of reinforced strongpoints which allowed his limited forces to control the handful of decent crossing points over the lake. However, after the lake froze solid in December, Rauch's strongpoints became terribly vulnerable. Two of the most important positions were Stützpunkt Zamoschenka (held by II/IR 415) and Stützpunkt Zales'ye (held by I/IR 415). Although these battalion-sized strongpoints were fairly well armed with light artillery and automatic weapons, they were more than 4 miles (6.5km) apart and unable to provide mutual support. However the southern part of Rauch's sector – roughly 20 miles wide – was held only by a thin screening force composed of two battalions of IR 416, two reconnaissance battalions and Sicherungs-Regiment 3. The junction between Heeresgruppe Nord and Heeresgruppe Mitte was held by the SS-Kavallerie-Brigade's reconnaissance battalion, which occupied a defensive position at the town of Peno, south of Ostashkov.

General-Colonel Purkaev's 3rd Shock Army quietly slipped into the Lake Seliger area in early January and assembled in the dense forests on the east side of the lake. Kurochkin succeeded in pulling off a relief in place without alerting the Germans, inserting Purkaev's army in the sector held by 27th Army and then that formation was briefly pulled out of the line and redesignated as 4th Shock Army. Soviet logistics were particularly poor in this area and many of the assault troops had not eaten for three days prior to the beginning of the counteroffensive. On the night of 8–9 January 1942, Purkaev sent several battalions of ski troops across Lake Seliger, aided by aerosans. The assault elements of 23rd, 33rd and 257th Rifle Divisions were not far behind. Rauch's troops were too thinly spread really to notice the beginning of the Soviet offensive until ski troops were detected near Stützpunkt Zales'ye. By the morning of 9 January, only 23rd Rifle Division was across in sufficient strength to make an attack on Stützpunkt Zamoschenka, but it was repulsed

with 170 dead. It took another day for Purkaev to get across Lake Seliger with the bulk of his shock groups and it was not until 10 January that he could mount a relatively coordinated attack by 23rd and 33rd Rifle Divisions against IR 415's strongpoints, while 20th Rifle Division conducted a fixing attack against IR 418. Neither attack succeeded, but the rest of 3rd Shock Army enjoyed greater success to the south, where 257th and 31st Rifle Divisions were able to push aside the German reconnaissance troops in front of them. Purkaev kept pounding on 123. Infanterie-Division's strongpoints, while his left-wing forces advanced steadily into the German rear. After several days of fighting, Rauch was forced to evacuate Stützpunkt Zales'ye. It was not long before the pursuing Soviets encircled Stützpunkt Zamoschenka as well and 23rd Rifle Division began a major night assault on this position at 0300hrs on 15 January, including tanks, artillery and plenty of infantry. The German garrison fired flares which illuminated the attackers 270yd (250m) short of the objective and then called in divisional artillery fire which succeeded in breaking up the Soviet attack. After this failure, the Soviets settled into a desultory siege of Stützpunkt Zamoschenka for the next week, but were hindered by shortages of artillery ammunition. Furthermore, bombardment from 76mm and 122mm guns proved unable to demolish the reinforced cellars that the Germans had built beneath the houses in the village.

Despite the difficulty in reducing German strongpoints, Purkaev's left wing made steady progress and by 15 January, 257th Rifle Division had advanced more than 20 miles towards Kholm. Rauch was forced to refuse his own extended flank to counter the Soviet penetration. Since 34th Army had launched only minor diversionary attacks against the rest of II AK, Brockdorff-Ahlefeldt ordered 32. Infanterie-Division to take over part of Rauch's sector while 12. Infanterie-Division sent a *Kampfgruppe* to help build up the new southern flank. By 21 January, the battered 123. Infanterie-Division had suffered 1,788 casualties and had barely 8,000–9,000 troops left, one-quarter of whom had frostbite. Although Hitler forbade it to retreat, 123. Infanterie-Division was being pounded by five Soviet divisions and had to retreat or face destruction. To obscure the retreat, Busch re-designated 123. Infanterie-Division as Gruppe Rauch and tried to reposition it to block the southern approaches to Demyansk. For his part, Purkaev split his army into three diverging groups; he sent 23rd Rifle Division and three rifle brigades northwards to push against the retreating Gruppe Rauch, while two divisions marched west towards Kholm and the rest of 3rd Shock Army turned south west towards Velikiye Luki. At a cost of about 4,000 dead, Purkaev had accomplished a complete breakthrough in his sector.

4th Shock Army attacks, 9–20 January 1942

General-Colonel Andrei Eremenko's 4th Shock Army had been massing around Ostashkov since early January, but he kept the worn-out units acquired from 27th Army in the front line up to the last minute in order to deceive the Germans. When the counteroffensive began on 9 January, Eremenko sent a shock group from 360th Rifle Division and two rifle brigades to rout 123. Infanterie-Division security forces in this sector, while the bulk of 4th Shock Army moved down the railway line towards its main objective, Toropets. At Peno – arguably one of the most important points on the entire Eastern Front in early January 1942 – the SS-Radfahr-Aufklärungsabteilung had only 614 troops with a few 75mm light infantry guns and 37mm anti-tank guns. The battalion was subordinate to XXIII AK in AOK 9 but the nearest German unit was over 5 miles (8km) away. On the morning of 10 January, a strong shock group from the relatively elite 249th Rifle Division and a company of T-34 tanks approached the town. At 1650hrs, the Soviet shock groups struck the SS cavalrymen at Peno and, within a matter of hours, the town was surrounded. The SS troopers managed to hold their own through most of the night but by the next morning their ammunition was nearly exhausted. After having suffered 30 per cent casualties, the SS troopers conducted a breakout through the Soviet ring and managed to escape southwards after abandoning much of their equipment. Local German army commanders grumbled that the SS troopers had retreated after less than a day's fighting, even though army-held strongpoints like Vzvad and Zamoschenka held for more than a week before yielding. Consequently, the survivors of the battalion were now placed under Busch's AOK 16 and he subordinated them to Infanterie-Regiment 189, which was just coming up the railway line from Toropets.

The OKH ordered Oberst Heinrich Hohmeyer's Infanterie-Regiment 189 to block the Soviet breakthrough as far from Toropets as possible, until more German reinforcements could arrive. Hohmeyer's command was nearly full strength and had three infantry battalions, a battalion of 10.5cm howitzers and a company of pioneers – about 3,800 men – but he was being asked to stop a 60,000-man shock army. His lead battalion had barely gone halfway to Peno when it encountered the advance elements of 249th Rifle Division

A German MG-34 team from 18. Infanterie-Division (mot.) firing from inside a building in Staraya Russa. X AK created a virtually impregnable urban defence within the city that fended off numerous Soviet attacks throughout 1941–43. Although Soviet artillery gradually reduced the urban centre to rubble, the North-western Front's failure to capture Staraya Russa played a large role in determining the outcome of the Demyansk campaign. (Ian Barter)

near Okhvat on 12 January. Hohmeyer decided to dig in and buy time for reinforcements to arrive in Toropets. The 249th Rifle Division immediately attacked, supported by a tank battalion, and was able to seize part of the village. The 189. Infanterie-Regiment suffered heavy losses but so had 249th Rifle Division, so Eremenko ordered his ski troops to bypass the German hedgehog. By 14 January, Hohmeyer's regiment was surrounded and he realized that the Soviets were pushing on to Toropets. Hohmeyer ordered a breakout attempt on 15 January but it quickly turned into a disaster and only 160 men from his regiment reached Toropets. Hohmeyer and an entire German regiment had been eliminated.

Despite Hohmeyer's gallant and futile sacrifice, the vanguard of 4th Shock Army reached Toropets on the morning of 20 January. The town was held by a motley group of 2,500 German troops, including the remnants of the SS reconnaissance battalion, two police companies and part of Wach-Bataillon 705. It did not take long for 249th Rifle Division, reinforced by two rifle brigades, to overcome this pathetic force and, by the next morning, the town and its valuable supplies had been captured intact. Eremenko's troops captured badly needed food and fuel in Toropets, which allowed their offensive to continue. He had advanced 40 miles (65km) in eight days and completely severed the connection between Heeresgruppe Nord and Heeresgruppe Mitte – the Wehrmacht was facing an unprecedented catastrophe. Yet temperatures were plunging ever lower in late January, falling to -32° F (-35° C) by 18 January and then -45° F (-43° C) by 24 January. Although the Germans suffered badly from the weather, the deep snow and freezing conditions also helped them by slowing the Soviet pursuit. After Toropets, Eremenko pushed south towards Velizh but his command was reassigned to Kalinin Front on 22 January and much of his subsequent operations lay outside the realm of the Demyansk–Kholm campaign.

CLOSING THE DEMYANSK POCKET, FEBRUARY 1942

Although 18. Infanterie-Division (mot.) had created a solid defence at Staraya Russa and 290. Infanterie-Division still held east of the Pola River, Morozov's 11th Army had succeeded in creating a 20-mile (32km) gap down the Red'ya Valley which now invited further exploitation southwards. As the lead elements of 1st GRC arrived near Staraya Russa, having marched 70 miles (110km) across the frozen marsh tracks from Valday, Morozov committed them piecemeal. On 2 February, he sent 14th and 15th Rifle Brigades southwards to seize the crossing over the Red'ya River at Davidovo. Not far behind, the reinforced 7th Guards Rifle Division also marched on Davidovo. Both Morozov and Kurochkin realized that Staraya Russa was too strong a position to storm, but they recognized that a golden opportunity now existed to encircle II AK at Demyansk. Since 2nd Shock Army's offensive on the Volkhov had stalled, there was less urgency for the North-western Front to press westwards and the Stavka authorized Kurochkin to redirect his offensive towards Demyansk.

At AOK 16 headquarters in Dno, Busch recognized the perilous situation facing II AK and he ordered the creation of several small Kampfgruppen to control critical road intersections, to prevent seizure by enemy partisans or paratroopers. Oberst Günter Leopold, commander of II/IR 368 from Scherer's

A German MG-34 heavy machine-gun team occupies a defensive position on the perimeter of the Demyansk pocket. Note that the German troops are well camouflaged for winter warfare and concealed by a tree line. (Ian Barter)

281. Sicherungs-Division was ordered to form one of these *Kampfgruppen*, to control the bridge at Davidovo on the Staraya Russa–Demyansk road. Initially, Leopold had only a few hundred troops but as the 11th Army breakthrough east of Staraya Russa increased, he was given part of II/IR 51 from 18. Infanterie-Division (mot.), some SS-'Totenkopf' motorcycle troopers, an artillery battery and two construction companies, for a total of 900 men. However, Kampfgruppe Leopold was given considerably more firepower than a standard German infantry battalion: three 105mm howitzers, three 75mm infantry guns, 11 81mm mortars, two 37mm PaK 36 guns and 53 machine guns. When the Soviet 15th Rifle Brigade approached the bridge at Davidovo on 3 February, Kampfgruppe Leopold repulsed it with heavy losses. However, the German defensive success was short lived. The lead elements of the experienced 7th Guards Rifle Division were not far behind, and 1st GRC managed to slip ski troops behind the German river defences. On 5 February, 1st GRC mounted a fairly well coordinated concentric attack from both sides of the river that nearly overwhelmed Kampfgruppe Leopold and forced it to abandon the bridge and retreat westwards. The 1st GRC promptly advanced south-east and captured the village of Ramushevo on the Lovat River on 8 February. Although II AK was not yet completely encircled, it was now isolated and totally dependent upon the Luftwaffe's airbridge for its supplies.

Although Kampfgruppe Leopold had been defeated, it bought vital time for Brockdorff-Ahlefeldt to transfer units westwards to protect the rear of II AK from the breakthrough by 1st GRC. He ordered Eicke to split the SS-'Totenkopf' Division into two regimental-sized *Kampfgruppen*; Eicke took the larger group to create a new *Stützpunkt* at Zeluch'ye on the road to Staraya Russa to cover the rear of the pocket, while Kampfgruppe Simon (comprising 1. SS-'Totenkopf' Regiment) was left to hold his division's sector – an extremely risky decision. The SS troopers rapidly moved to Zeluch'ye and dug in. Since Gruppe Rauch, the remnants of the routed 123. Infanterie-Division, was having difficulty holding the southern side of the Demyansk salient near Molvetitsy, Brockdorff-Ahlefeldt also ordered the lightly engaged 12. Infanterie-Division to transfer a reinforced *Kampfgruppe* to hold the sector between Gruppe Rauch and 32. Infanterie-Division. However, Gruppe Rauch's right flank was hanging in the air, with only a few small blocking detachments deployed west of Molvetitsy. On the northern side of the

Creation of the Demyansk pocket, 5 February to 20 March 1942

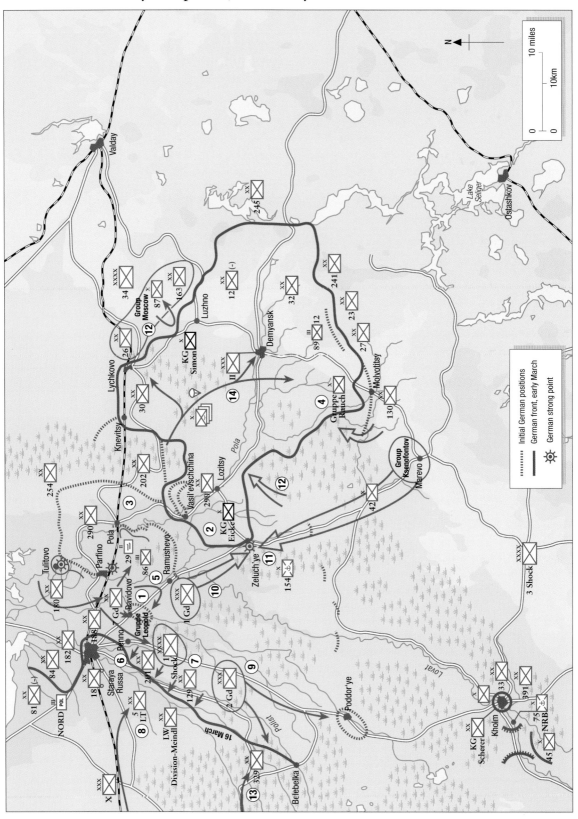

Demyansk salient, 290. Infanterie-Division was virtually surrounded and Soviet ski troops were operating freely in its rear. Brockdorff-Ahlefeldt accepted that the division had fought a valiant defensive stand but it had already suffered 1,400 casualties in four weeks of fighting and if it was annihilated he would lack the manpower to hold the northern part of the Demyansk salient. He was able to get permission from Busch to abandon Pola and allow 290. Infanterie-Division to retreat southwards to tie in with Gruppe Eicke at Zeluch'ye.

While 1st GRC continued to press south-east across the Lovat, Kurochkin took measures to widen the gap between the isolated II AK in Demyansk and X AK forces around Staraya Russa. He directed the newly arrived 2nd GRC to eliminate the German blocking positions at Chirikova and Penno, then push west to the Polist. On 8 February, two rifle brigades from 2nd GRC attacked and captured Penno and then with the assistance of the elite 8th Guards Rifle Division, 2nd GRC pushed west and south-west. The only German blocking units in the area were Kampfgruppe Mayer along the Polist and Kampfgruppe Sperling near Poddor'ye, but neither could do more than delay the Soviet steamroller. Although Kuznetsov's 1st Shock Army had been transferred to the North-western Front from the Western Front in order to complete the capture of Staraya Russa, Kurochkin decided to commit it to the south as well. Once 1st Shock Army had assembled south of Staraya Russa on 12 February, it joined the efforts of 1st and 2nd GRC to widen the Soviet breach between the Polist and Lovat rivers. For the next three weeks, 1st Shock Army and 2nd GRC slowly pushed westwards across the Polist River, threatening to encircle Staraya Russa from the south, but the lack of roads in the swampy terrain reduced the Soviet steamroller to a crawl. Busch desperately pleaded with the OKH for reinforcements for X AK, arguing that if he could not hold the Polist line that it would be impossible to re-open the road to Demyansk. Hitler authorized the transfer of three new divisions from Germany and another from the quiet Leningrad sector. The lead elements of 5. leichte-Division began arriving in mid-February, just in time to slow down 1st Shock Army.

With the defeat of Kampfgruppe Leopold, Kurochkin now felt that the time was ripe to complete the encirclement of II AK at Demyansk. He ordered 1st GRC to conduct a converging attack towards Zeluch'ye to complete the encirclement by linking up with 3rd Shock Army's Group Ksenofontov, which now belonged to the Kalinin Front. The 1st GRC had 7th Guards Rifle Division, 42nd Rifle Brigade and 154th Naval Rifle Brigade across the Lovat, while Purkaev's 3rd Shock Army had two rifle divisions and three rifle

1 5 February, 7th Guards Rifle Division (1st GRC) attacks Gruppe Leopold *Stützpunkt* on Red'ya River.

2 5 February, Gruppe Eicke forms *Stützpunkt* at Zeluch'ye with part of SS-'Totenkopf', leaving Kampfgruppe Simon to hold a division-sized sector at Luzhno.

3 6 February, 290. Infanterie Division is under heavy pressure in exposed salient, with Soviet ski troops penetrating the unprotected south-west part of the salient. X AK authorizes the division to withdraw southwards to Vasil'evschchina.

4 Gruppe Rauch is barely able to hold the southern sector against pressure from 3rd Shock Army.

5 8 February, 7th Guards Rifle Division captures Ramushevo.

6 8 February, the 2nd GRC captures Penno.

7 12 February, 1st Shock Army arrives south of Staraya Russa and begins pushing westwards to the Polist River against weak

resistance from Luftwaffe-Division Meindl.

8 15–19 February, 5. leichte Infanterie-Division arrives to block 1st Shock Army advance across Polist River.

9 2nd Guards Rifle Corps continues to advance south-west along Polist River.

10 20 February, North-western Front begins concentric attack with 1st GRC and Group Ksenofontov to complete encirclement of II AK in Demyansk.

11 25 February, Soviet link-up near Zeluch'ye creates the Demyansk pocket.

12 6–10 March, attacks by Group Ksenofontov and Group Moscow fail to crack outer perimeter of Demyansk pocket.

13 12 March, 329. Infanterie-Division begins arriving from Germany.

14 6–23 March, Soviet airborne infiltration attack fails to destroy the pocket.

brigades around Mareva. Both formations were spread thinly on the ground and could commit only brigade-sized shock groups to the new effort. The 37th Rifle Brigade spearheaded the main push from the north and 154th Naval Rifle Brigade and 42nd Rifle Brigade led the attack from the south. Although the SS troopers were able to prevent 1st GRC from making much progress, the two brigades from 3rd Shock Army advanced fairly quickly against spotty German resistance and were able to link up with the North-western Front troops south of Zeluch'ye on 25 February, thereby creating the Demyansk pocket. For the first time in World War II, a major German formation was surrounded and faced with annihilation. Hitler responded by declaring Demyansk a *Festung* (fortress) and ordering Busch to prepare a relief operation as soon as possible.

On the same day as the troops from 1st GRC and 3rd Shock Army accomplished their link-up, the Stavka issued new orders to Kurochkin that the North-western Front would crush the Demyansk pocket within four to five days. The 1st GRC began a series of violent attacks against Gruppe Eicke at Zeluch'ye. Eicke had roughly 4,000 troops to fight off 7th Guards Rifle Division, several rifle brigades and a variety of ski battalions. The SS troops managed to hold onto Zeluch'ye and inflict crippling losses on 1st GRC, but suffered about 60 per cent losses themselves. By the thinnest of margins, the Germans prevented the Soviets from overrunning the thinly manned western part of the pocket in late February.

While the fight at Zeluch'ye continued, the Stavka decided to assign the mission of reducing the pocket entirely to the North-western Front and temporarily transferred the two rifle divisions and five rifle brigades from Group Ksenofontov that were on the west side of the Demyansk pocket to Kurochkin's command. Given sole responsibility for reducing the pocket, Kurochkin quickly developed an elaborate plan to crush the Demyansk pocket in a matter of days. Recognizing that the Luftwaffe airlift was critical for the combat effectiveness of II AK, Kurochkin proposed to directly attack the three airfields around Demyansk by means of ground infiltration. Accepting Kurochkin's assessment, the Stavka duly provided him with 8,500 paratroopers from 1st Airborne Corps at Moscow to conduct the deep attack. Kurochkin intended the paratroopers to infiltrate the pocket over the course of a week, one brigade at a time, and then launch a coordinated attack on the airfields in conjunction with conventional attacks by 34th Army, 1st GRC and Group Ksenofontov on the exterior of the pocket. Hit simultaneously from within and without, with its supplies disrupted, Kurochkin reckoned that II AK would collapse like a house of cards.

Prior to the infiltration, a single battalion of 204th Airborne Brigade was parachuted north-west of Demyansk over the course of four nights. This unit was expected to establish landing zones and a logistic base near the target in order to resupply the main body when it arrived. The infiltration began on the night of 6 March, with 1st Airborne Brigade slipping through the frozen swamps in the north-west corner of the pocket, between 30. and 290. Infanterie-Divisionen. Although the first brigade conducted a successful infiltration, the Germans detected its movement and were on their guard for the next unit. When 204th Airborne Brigade began advancing through the swamps a few nights later, it came under heavy German artillery fire which inflicted 30 per cent casualties. The final unit, 2nd Airborne Brigade, was also pummelled by German artillery fire. Nevertheless, both 1st and 204th Airborne Brigades were able to assemble in the base camp north of Demyansk by 14 March, while 2nd Brigade split off to attack the rear of 30. Infanterie-Division at Lychkovo. Despite the daring nature of this infiltration attack, it was soon apparent that Soviet logistic support was totally inadequate. The paratroopers had been given only three days' worth of rations but spent more than a week marching through deep snow to their objectives. Owing to numerous small firefights en route, much of their ammunition was expended as well. Soviet aerial resupply failed to get more than token amounts of supplies to the paratroopers and thus, the assault force was hungry and low on ammunition. Nevertheless, on the evening of 19 March 1st and 204th Airborne Brigades mounted an attack on the two airstrips north of Demyansk. However, the forfeiture of surprise enabled II AK to shift part of Kampfgruppe Simon from SS-'Totenkopf' to defend the airfields. Consequently, the Soviet ground assaults were repulsed with heavy losses. Similarly, 2nd Airborne Brigade's attack on Lychkovo, timed to coincide with a frontal assault on 30. Infanterie-Division by 34th Army, also failed. Unable to capture the airfields, the survivors of the airborne brigades retreated south, hoping to reach 3rd

German troops wait to fly into Demyansk during the winter airlift. Thanks to the success of the airbridge, II AK received a steady stream of replacements to replenish its combat losses. Note that these troops seem well equipped for winter warfare. (Nik Cornish at Stavka)

RUSSIAN PARATROOPERS ATTACK DOBROSLI AIRSTRIP VERSUS KAMPFGRUPPE SIMON, 19 MARCH 1942 (pp. 50–51)

In early March 1942, the Soviet North-western Front decided to make a bold attempt to collapse the Demyansk pocket from within by infiltrating three elite airborne brigades into the poorly guarded north-west side of the pocket, then to attack the two airfields near Demyansk upon which II AK depended for survival. Colonel-Lieutenant Nikolay E. Tarasov's 1st Airborne Brigade infiltrated through German lines on the evening of 6 March, followed by 204th Airborne Brigade. The Soviet paratroopers carried only light weapons and moved on skis to an assembly area north of Demyansk.

However, the Germans had detected the Soviet infiltration and II AK ordered Kampfgruppe Simon, led by SS-Oberführer Max Simon, to send several companies of his 'Totenkopf' troopers to protect the two airstrips at Globovshchina and Dobrosli. The Soviet paratroopers were not ready to mount a coordinated assault on the airstrips until the evening of 19 March. This scene depicts the attack on Dobrosli, when over 3,000 Soviet paratroopers from 1st Airborne Brigade **(1)** and part of 204th

Airborne Brigade emerged from the wood line north of the airstrip and attacked the Waffen-SS positions protecting the airstrip **(2)** (no aircraft were on the flight line at night, but there were large stockpiles of supplies). If the airstrips could be captured, the Luftwaffe airlift would have to be halted and the Soviets expected German morale inside the pocket to collapse.

Although the SS troopers were outnumbered about 8:1 at Dobrosli, they had the advantage of prepared positions and fire support. German machine-gunners cut swaths through the lead wave of attacking paratroopers, while 82mm mortars fired high explosive and illumination rounds **(3)** to assist the defenders. Nevertheless, Tarasov's paratroopers kept on coming and at least one company reached the German positions and engaged the 'Totenkopf' troopers in hand-to-hand fighting. After desperate close-quarter fighting, the Soviet paratroopers fell back into the woods, having left over 600 dead behind. The raid was a costly failure and over the next week, Kampfgruppe Simon harried the retreating paratroopers to near annihilation.

Shock Army. Kampfgruppe Simon harried the retreating paratroopers, overrunning their supply base and gradually smashing each isolated detachment in turn. By the end of March, barely 900 survivors of the 8,500-man 1st Airborne Corps had reached Soviet lines, with the rest dead or captured. Furthermore, all the Soviet attacks around the western and northern periphery of the Demyansk pocket had been repulsed. The Soviet North-western Front's Winter Counteroffensive had culminated, with its combat power no longer sufficient to overcome the isolated II AK.

Inside the Demyansk pocket, the survival of II AK depended upon adequate supplies of food and ammunition, but the outlook was grim. Once the pocket was formed, Brockdorff-Ahlefeldt ordered his troops to seize food from local Russian civilians, which caused widespread starvation. Despite these measures, by the end of January 1942 rations for troops within the pocket had been cut by one-third; the daily ration was typically 1¼oz (36g) of dried vegetables and 2oz (60g) of horse meat. Some troops were reduced to eating oats reserved for the horses. Ammunition was also running low and was being consumed at an alarming rate.

THE AIRLIFT, FEBRUARY–MAY 1942

Even before the North-western Front succeeded in completing its encirclement of the Demyansk pocket, it became increasingly difficult for AOK 16 to supply six divisions with 96,000 troops and 20,000 horses along a single dirt road from the Staraya Russa railhead. Heeresgruppe Nord had already been requesting air resupply missions from Luftflotte I for some time and two transport groups – I./KGzbV 172 and KGrzbV 9 – were supplementing the inadequate logistic network of AOK 16 with regular deliveries into Demyansk's snow-packed airfield. However, these two groups had barely 30 operational Ju-52s by early January 1942 and their combined delivery capacity was at best 60 tons per day. When the Demyansk pocket was created and II AK informed the Luftwaffe that it needed a minimum of 300 tons of supplies delivered by air per day (including 54 tons of food and 21 tons of fuel), it was clear that Luftflotte I would need significant help to accomplish this mission. Initially, the airlift was a disorganized failure, with only 16 tons delivered on 9 February and 27 tons on 10 February.

On 18 February, Oberst Fritz Morzik, the Luftwaffe's *Lufttransportführer* (Air Transport Chief) arrived at Pskov-South airbase to take personal control of the first major airlift operation in military history. Morzik started with virtually nothing, having a staff of only nine men and a single field telephone but he immediately requested the Luftwaffe to transfer five more transport groups to his command. These aircraft began arriving from Vitebsk and Orsha, providing Morzik with another 60–70 operational aircraft, with more on the way. Morzik then began establishing rudimentary air traffic control parties at Demyansk. The sub-zero weather was a severe handicap since aircraft serviceability rates were reduced to about 30 per cent and engine maintenance was impossible on open forward strips in -40° F (-40° C) temperatures. Rubber tyres cracked and even oil and gas lines froze solid and the airlift would have failed if the Luftwaffe had not introduced the 'cold-start method' of increasing oil viscosity. Morzik's staff became masters of improvisation, begging and borrowing skilled technicians, spare parts and warming trucks from all over the Third Reich.

At first, the VVS-North-western Front ignored the airlift and kept its limited forces focused on providing ground support, mostly to 3rd Shock Army. Morzik had his transport groups flying primarily from Pskov and Ostrov to Demyansk, a distance of 155–160 miles (250–260km) or about 90 minutes of flight time. He instructed the transports to fly in at treetop level in groups of two–three planes. Since each Ju-52 brought in about 2 tons of supplies and Morzik soon had over 200 transports involved in the airlift, he was just able to satisfy the minimum logistic requirements for II AK. However, ground facilities at Demyansk were primitive and the army was reluctant to supply troops for unloading at first because they needed every man at the front. Nevertheless, these problems were gradually resolved and the airlift succeeded in getting just enough food, fuel, ammunition and replacements through to keep II AK in the fight. By the end of February 1942, Morzik had received another five transport groups and in early March he received three more culled from flight schools in Germany, giving him more than half of Germany's fleet of Ju-52 transports. The Luftwaffe also sent Ju-86 and Fw-200 Condor aircraft to participate in the airlift.

It was not long, however, before the VVS noticed the airlift and made a concerted effort to interfere. Within days, lone Soviet fighters began picking off Ju-52 transports bound for Demyansk and more than a dozen were lost by the end of February. Soviet bombers also began regular attacks on Demyansk's two airstrips, causing further losses and disruption. Luftflotte I had too few Bf-109 fighters to secure air superiority over Demyansk but air-to-air combat increased over the pocket in March; Luftflotte I claimed 162 Soviet aircraft over this area in March, but lost 52 Ju-52 transports. Soviet flak was also becoming problematic on the approach route, causing damage to low-flying transports. The arrival of the thaw in late March also presented problems as Demyansk's airstrips turned into waterlogged bogs. Belatedly, the Stavka recognized the importance of interdicting the Demyansk airlift and in early April it transferred 6th Strike Aviation Group (UAG) with six fighter regiments to augment VVS-North-western Front. The arrival of 6th UAG enabled the VVS seriously to contest the airspace over Demyansk and inflicted great damage on the Luftwaffe airlift. The Luftwaffe also transferred more fighters to Luftflotte 1, which enabled the airlift to continue, albeit with significant attrition. Morzik decided it was time to change his tactics, ordering his transport groups to fly in larger groups, sometimes with a few escort fighters, and at altitudes of 6,000–8,000ft (1,850–2,500m) above the flak. Owing to these changed tactics and more fighter protection, Luftflotte I managed to keep the losses of Ju-52s down to only eight aircraft in April,

The Luftwaffe airlift, January–May 1942

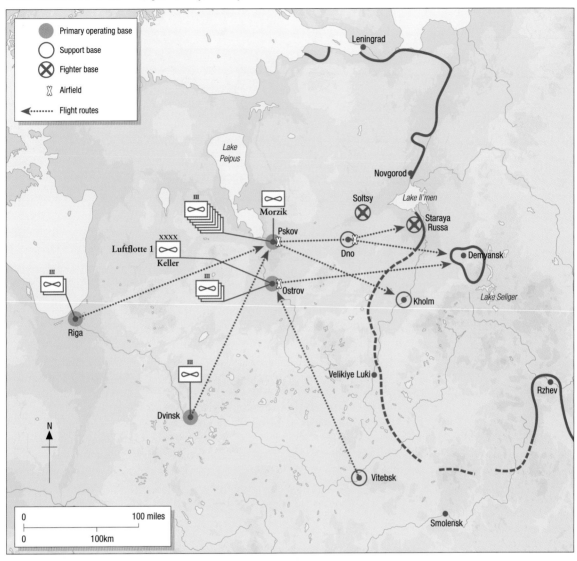

but claimed over 260 Soviet aircraft. On the other side, the VVS-North-western Front failed to make a single attack on Morzik's bases such as Pskov or Ostrov, which might have severely disrupted the airlift.

The airlift proved sufficient to keep II AK in a reasonable state of combat effectiveness. Food stocks were gradually built up to a four to five day stockpile, but distribution to front-line troops was far from satisfactory. Hay and oats for the horses was another story though, with many horses suffering from malnutrition that thinned their ranks. It was not until 4 March that the Luftwaffe was able to reach the 300-ton-per-day requirement. Eventually, Morzik's fliers were able to exceed the daily quota and the largest amount of supplies delivered in any one day was 544 tons. However, the greatest demand came for artillery ammunition, with up to 80–100 tons being used per day. A single 15cm battery could fire off one ton of ammunition in less than two minutes. By early March 1942, artillery batteries were reduced to 30 per cent of their normal basic load. Interestingly, the SS-'Totenkopf'

Division was responsible for consuming about 50 per cent of the artillery ammunition used by the entire II AK during the airlift. Morzik's transports also brought in replacements and equipment. The 123. and 290. Infanterie-Divisionen were particularly depleted, but German industry could not provide sufficient weapons to re-equip these units, so captured weapons were substituted. The Luftwaffe provided II AK with 147 Soviet DP light machine guns and ten 45mm anti-tank guns, which eased resupply since the defenders could use captured ammunition for these weapons.

Morzik also had to keep Scherer's garrison in Kholm supplied as well. Although the supply requirements of Kampfgruppe Scherer were much less than II AK's, Kholm's tiny 540yd (500m) airstrip was under fire from almost the beginning of the siege. One of the last Ju-52s taking off from the strip before the ring closed, loaded with wounded soldiers, received a direct hit from artillery fire. Pressured by the OKL staff in Berlin, Morzik made a desperate attempt to land seven Ju-52s from KGrzbV 9 at Kholm on 25 February, which succeeded in delivering some badly needed ammunition but lost four more aircraft in the process. Supply runs to Kholm were far more hazardous than Demyansk and 27 Ju-52s were lost before Kholm was relieved in May 1942. Afterwards, Morzik resorted to using parachute-delivered supplies and gliders to supply Kholm.

By the time that ground communications with Kholm and Demyansk were regained in May 1942, Luftflotte I had flown 14,455 air transport sorties into the pockets. A total of 24,303 tons of supplies and equipment, as well as 15,446 replacements, were flown into the pockets and 22,093 wounded were flown out. However, the cost was exceedingly high; 125 aircraft were lost (106 Ju-52s, 17 He-111s and two Ju-86s) in the airlift, another 140 were badly damaged and 387 aircrew were killed. This loss rate equates to nearly half the transport planes Germany built in 1942. Furthermore, it is often missed that the Demyansk airlift did not cease when the German relief operations restored ground communications. In mid-May 1942, two-thirds of II AK's minimum daily supply requirements were still being delivered by Luftflotte I and only 50–100 tons per day were reaching Demyansk through the Ramushevo corridor. The only saving grace for the Germans was that spring weather allowed the Luftwaffe to deliver more supplies with fewer aircraft and Morzik released all but three transport groups back to their original commands. Another 18,639 transport sorties were flown into Demyansk after the Ramushevo corridor was opened and few people realize that the Demyansk airlift was still ongoing when the Stalingrad airlift began six months later. It was the inability of the Luftwaffe to conduct two concurrent major airlift operations that finally caused Hitler to reconsider his decision to hold the Demyansk salient. Although the airlift saved II AK and the Kholm garrison, Morzik later regarded it as a failure since it encouraged Hitler to hold onto hopeless positions instead of making tactical withdrawals. The Demyansk–Kholm airlifts also had two major negative operational impacts on the Luftwaffe. Firstly, the transfer of flight training cadres from Germany severely disrupted the Luftwaffe's flight training programme. Secondly, the consumption of 42,155 tons of aviation fuel – roughly one-third of the Third Reich's production of aviation fuel for one month – was an exorbitant waste of fuel that the Luftwaffe would later regret.

THE SIEGE OF KHOLM, JANUARY–MAY 1942

Prior to the war, Kholm had been a quiet town of about 10,000 people. Even after the Germans occupied the town in August 1941, Kholm had remained a quiet backwater. Generalmajor Theodor Scherer came to Kholm with elements of his 281. Sicherungs-Division in the autumn of 1941 in an effort to control the growing partisan presence in the surrounding woods. Yet most of his division was scattered far and wide across the II AK area, leaving few troops actually in Kholm. When Soviet 3rd Army shattered 123. Infanterie-Division's screen line along Lake Seliger on 15 January 1942, Kholm suddenly assumed great importance as a vital road junction. If 3rd Shock Army seized it, they could quickly penetrate into AOK 16's unguarded rear areas. Scherer himself was in Loknya, 45 miles (72km) south-west of Kholm, when the crisis began to develop and the only German troops in Kholm were a single company of Landesschützen-Bataillon 869 and construction troops from Bau-Bataillon 680.

The monument to the Soviet 154th Naval Rifle Brigade at Tsemena. The naval infantrymen played a key role in closing the Demyansk pocket in February 1942, but they paid a very heavy price. Over 500 from this brigade are listed as killed in action during the Demyansk campaign. (PhilCurme)

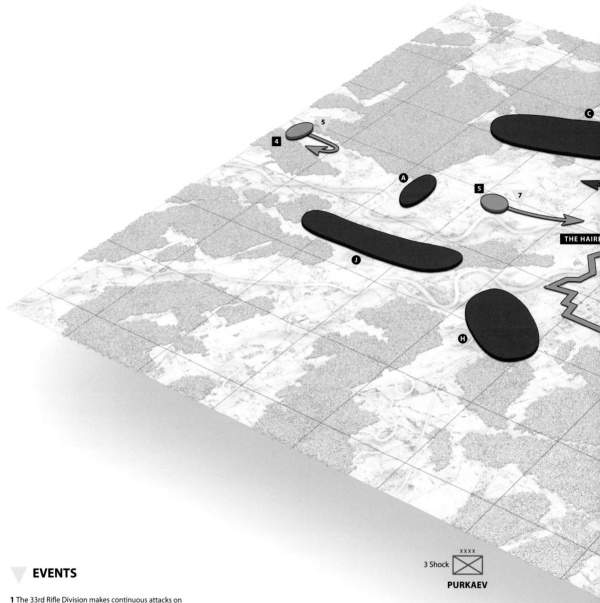

THE HAIR

C

A

J

5

4

5

7

H

xxxx
3 Shock

PURKAEV

▼ EVENTS

1 The 33rd Rifle Division makes continuous attacks on the eastern perimeter of Kholm beginning in January and continuing through 1 May.

2 The 164th Rifle Regiment arrives in early February and seizes part of northern Kholm.

3 The airstrip is put out of action by Soviet artillery fire.

4 A landing zone for gliders is created on the frozen river.

5 Gruppe Uckermann tries several times in February and March to break through to Kholm but is blocked by 75th Naval Rifle Brigade, which is reinforced by 42nd Rifle Brigade.

6 Elements of 2nd GRC, occupy positions north-west of Kholm in April.

7 Gruppe Lang fights its way into Kholm, 5 May.

THE BATTLE FOR KHOLM, 9 JANUARY TO 5 MAY 1942

Entirely surrounded, Kampfgruppe Scherer holds out against superior Soviet forces.

58

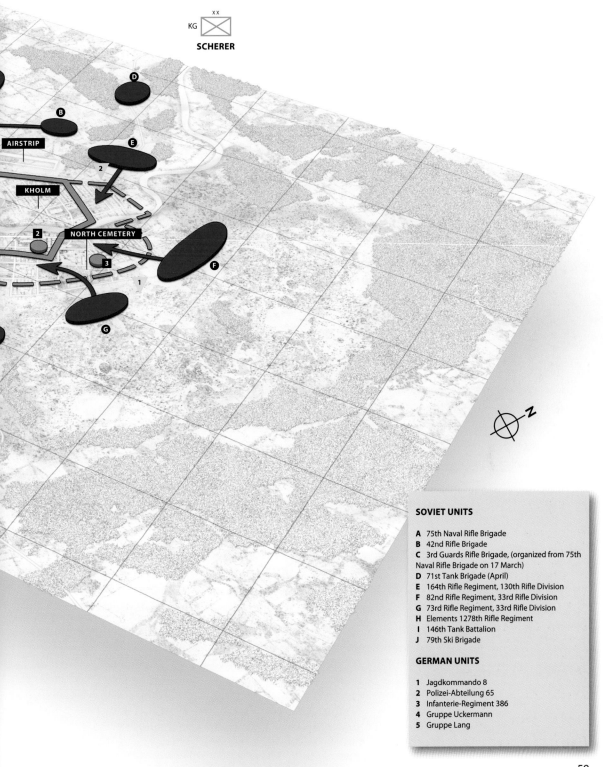

Note: Gridlines are shown at intervals of 1 km/0.62 miles

KG XX SCHERER

AIRSTRIP

KHOLM

NORTH CEMETERY

SOVIET UNITS

A 75th Naval Rifle Brigade
B 42nd Rifle Brigade
C 3rd Guards Rifle Brigade, (organized from 75th Naval Rifle Brigade on 17 March)
D 71st Tank Brigade (April)
E 164th Rifle Regiment, 130th Rifle Division
F 82nd Rifle Regiment, 33rd Rifle Division
G 73rd Rifle Regiment, 33rd Rifle Division
H Elements 1278th Rifle Regiment
I 146th Tank Battalion
J 79th Ski Brigade

GERMAN UNITS

1 Jagdkommando 8
2 Polizei-Abteilung 65
3 Infanterie-Regiment 386
4 Gruppe Uckermann
5 Gruppe Lang

Policeman's Ravine on the north-east corner of Kholm. This sector was originally held by troops from Reserve-Polizei-Abteilung 65, but 3rd Shock Army was able to gain a foothold in Kholm by infiltrating this ravine. (Phil Curme)

Oberst Christoph Stengel, commander of IR 416 from 123. Infanterie-Division, led the retreat from the southern end of Lake Seliger and was the first senior German officer to arrive in Kholm on 16 January. In addition to his own two battalions with 1,200–1,500 troops, Stengel was soon joined by a company from 53. Reserve-Polizei-Abteilung and the entire 65. Reserve-Polizei-Abteilung. Not only were Stengel's troops exhausted and many suffering from frostbite, but they had abandoned most of their heavy weapons in the retreat. Stengel immediately took command of all these units and established a defence just east of the town to delay Purkaev's pursuing troops, while radioing to AOK 16 for reinforcements. However, the single road to Loknya was barely trafficable because of deep snow and intense partisan activity, so the prospects for immediate help were poor.

Meanwhile, Scherer was gathering up reinforcements for Kholm while trying to get to the town with his own staff. Generalmajor Horst Freiherr von Uckermann's 218. Infanterie-Division had been enjoying quiet coastal defence duty in Denmark for nearly a year when it was suddenly notified in early January 1942 to transfer to Riga. The division was still en route when the Soviet Winter Counteroffensive began but Busch dispatched the lead elements to buttress the disintegrating right flank of AOK 16. One of the first units to detrain at Loknya was the headquarters of IR 386 under Oberstleutnant Johannes Manitius, and I/IR 386, which Scherer promptly sent to Kholm on 16 January in every available truck. He also dispatched supply trucks with 20,000 rations and 13,000 rounds of small arms ammunition. The rest of IR 386 and the III/Artillerie-Regiment 218 would follow in a few days, once more transport was available. Scherer and his staff went with Manitius, leaving Uckermann to assemble the rest of his division at Loknya. Busch ordered Uckermann to move to Kholm and take charge of the defence as soon as possible.

Yet even as Scherer headed towards Kholm, the Soviets were already making their play for the town. Vatutin, the North-western Front chief of staff, intended to use Nikolas G. Vasilyev's 2nd Leningrad Partisan Brigade to seize Kholm in a *coup de main* before German reinforcements arrived.

Vasilyev was a political commissar who had been sent by the North-western Front to organize partisans behind German lines in August 1941 and he maintained radio contact with front headquarters. During the night of 17–18 January, Vasilyev led about 800 of his well-armed partisans into Kholm from three directions, penetrating the thin German security perimeter. Some German sentries were quietly eliminated and the garrison was not fully aware of the threat until Vasilyev's men launched a full-scale attack on the German headquarters at 0400hrs on 18 January. The Germans were caught completely by surprise the town commandant was among those killed. In addition, their entire truck park was destroyed. The fighting continued for hours until the partisans ran low on ammunition and decided to break off the fight. Soviet sources claimed hundreds of Germans were killed or wounded against only 52 partisan casualties. A number of partisans stayed behind in the town as snipers, but were eventually found and hanged by vengeful SS policemen. If 3rd Shock Army had arrived when expected, Kholm would have been lost.

TOP
A German alarm unit inside Kholm awaits the order to counterattack a Soviet penetration. Taking advantage of the central position, Scherer created small reserve units that he could shuffle around the perimeter to retake any position that fell to Soviet assault. (Author's collection)

BOTTOM
Dead Soviet soldiers stacked in a pile on the outskirts of Kholm. The 3rd Shock Army continued to attack Kholm using the same unimaginative tactics day after day, which enabled Kampfgruppe Scherer to become quite proficient in chopping these infantry-heavy assaults to pieces with mortar and machine-gun fire. Soviet personnel losses at Kholm were horrendous. (Bundesarchiv, Bild 101I-004-3635-20A, Fotograf: Richard Muck)

FIGHT TO THE LAST HAND GRENADE, KHOLM, 0105HRS 24 MARCH 1942 (pp. 62–63)

Kampfgruppe Scherer was first surrounded in Kholm by Soviet 3rd Shock Army on 21 January 1942. Over the next eight weeks, Scherer's men repulsed dozens of Soviet attacks, day after day. However, they were increasingly weakened by the severe cold and, even worse, the Luftwaffe's daily supply drops were not keeping up with the constant consumption. By mid-March, the German defenders were living on one-third rations and were running out of ammunition.

On the afternoon of 23 March, 33rd Rifle Division launched an all-out attack from the south side of town, with both infantry and tanks. The Soviet assault groups pushed fanatically towards the GPU building, ignoring casualties. In order to conserve ammunition, Scherer's machine-gunners allowed the Soviet infantry to get within point-blank range before opening fire, and then they cut down the clumps of Soviet infantry. Both sides traded grenades back and forth, from opposite sides of the street. However, the Germans had particular difficulty dealing with the Soviet tanks, since they were very short of anti-tank weapons and ammunition. A small number of the new

Stielgranaten 41 hollow-charge grenades for the 37mm PaK 36 **(1)** had been flown into Kholm and they succeeded in knocking out several of the light T-60 tanks. However these rounds were soon expended and the anti-tank guns fell silent, enabling a number of T-34 tanks to advance boldly into the town. One T-34 **(2)** made it to the GPU building **(3)** and began firing into it from outside, killing many defenders. Reduced to close-quarter weapons, Scherer's men dropped concentrated charges **(4)** and Teller mines onto Soviet tanks from upper storeys of buildings.

Around 0105hrs, Scherer reported to XXXIX AK that the last hand grenade had been used and that heavy fighting had been going on for 11 hours around the GPU building. He desperately requested the Luftwaffe to drop more ammunition into the Kholm pocket. Yet when daylight arrived, the fighting had finally subsided and the area around the GPU was littered with dead bodies and burning tanks, but the building was still in German hands. Kampfgruppe Scherer had survived another night in Kholm.

Shortly after this attack subsided, Scherer arrived in Kholm with Manitius' column, which added another 1,000 troops to the garrison. Amazingly, Jagdkommando 8 (Gebirgs) also marched overland into Kholm from the north that day on snowshoes. Scherer took command of the 3,158 German troops in the town and continued the ad hoc effort to fortify the town, although no mines or barbed wire were available. Hitler promptly designated Kholm as a *Festung* (fortress), which meant that evacuation was not an option. Although the German historian Paul Carrell, formerly a senior SS official, tried to create the myth that Kholm was 'a fortress without artillery', in fact the garrison had three 75mm infantry guns, as well as 18 mortars. Later, it would receive a number of 3.7cm, 4.2cm and 5cm PaK guns delivered by glider. Scherer realized that Kholm was an excellent defensive position, sitting on a high bluff with superb fields of fire. A number of large stone buildings, such as the former GPU prison on the south-east side of town, provided the defenders with excellent cover.

Meanwhile, General-Major Aleksandr K. Makarev's 33rd Rifle Division was approaching Kholm through deep snow from due east with orders to take the town at once. After their 70-mile (110km) pursuit of the shattered 123. Infanterie-Division, Makarev's division arrived piecemeal began pushing in Stengel's reauguards east of the town. At 0200hrs on 21 January, Makarev attacked Kholm with elements of three regiments from the north, west and south-west. Makarev's troops gained inroads into the town, but Scherer's improvised defense just held, albeit at the cost of 52 dead and most of his ammunition expended. Afterwards, Makarev threw a ring around the town to prevent any more German reinforcements from arriving. Although the Soviets claimed to have Kholm surrounded, Makarev had to split his division with two regiments probing the town and one regiment to block the road from Loknya. In fact, the Soviet encirclement of Kholm was very tenuous for several weeks and Uckermann's relief column was able to slip some reinforcements, including two companies of IR 386 and 130 men from Maschinengewehr-Bataillon 10 past Makarev's roadblocks into the town between 25 and 28 January. However, Uckermann's small relief force consisted of only 1,000 troops and it could not hold open the road to Kholm and Makarev's troops finally clamped the trap shut around Kholm by 28 January. The Luftwaffe began resupply flights into Kholm the next day, which Makarev could not effectively prevent since he lacked artillery or flak initially. Between 29 January and 1 February, Luftwaffe Ju-52 transports made 42 landings at Kholm's tiny airstrip and flew out 379 wounded.

After the failure of his first attack on 21 January, Makarev continued aggressive infantry probes into Kholm. Both sides had limited artillery support, mostly light field guns and mortars. However, Makarev relied upon a small number of tanks to spearhead assaults into the northern and south-western sections of Kholm and was able to gain some ground. Throughout 24–26 January, Kampfgruppe Scherer was under intense pressure from constant Soviet attacks, which continued even at night. Close combat became the norm in Kholm, with grenades becoming the weapon of choice. Since the town was surrounded by a layer of hip-dip snow and wide open areas, the Soviets tended to keep attacking along the same axis, which made their actions predictable. The Soviet 164th Rifle Regiment succeeded in capturing Kholm's airstrip, but Scherer's troops were able to regain it with a desperate counterattack. Scherer called frantically for the Luftwaffe to bomb Makarev's shock groups, but Stuka support in the opening stages of the battle for Kholm

When Kholm was surrounded, Heeresgruppe Nord sent Kampfgruppe Crissoli from 8. Panzer-Division to augment the relief effort. The *Kampfgruppe* was equipped with PzKpfw III medium tanks with short-barrel 50mm guns, which were no match for Soviet T-34 or KV-1 tanks. When 3rd Shock Army deployed 2 T-34 tanks on the approach road to Kholm, Kampfgruppe Crissoli was brought to an abrupt halt and its commander was wounded. (Nik Cornish at Stavka)

was rare due to weather conditions. Scherer also demanded help from Kampfgruppe Uckermann, but it had insufficient strength to break Makarev's encirclement. During the fighting, fire spread to warehouses holding half the garrison's food supplies, which were destroyed. Yet after that, Scherer's troops dug their heels in inside their tight mile-wide (2km) perimeter and yielded little ground over the next three months. Throughout late January, the fighting in Kholm involved mostly close-range infantry combat and losses were heavy on both sides. Kampfgruppe Scherer suffered over 500 casualties in a week of fighting. However, Makarev's division was also burnt out, with two of its regiments reduced to fewer than 300 troops each, but the Stavka ordered attacks to continue.

Makarev pounded away at the south-east corner of town, but until mid-February Kampfgruppe Scherer was neither substantially outnumbered nor outgunned. Once Purkaev recognized that Makarev could not take Kholm with a single battle-weary division, he sent him the fresh 391st Rifle Division, 146th Tank Battalion (two T-34 and 11 T-60s), 44th Artillery Regiment (76mm guns) and three BM-8 multiple rocket launchers. This meant about 23,000 Soviet troops were besieging 4,500 Germans at Kholm – theoretically a 5:1 advantage. On 13 February, Soviet artillery began a sustained bombardment and the VVS conducted bombing sorties which together, steadily reduced much of the town to rubble. Two Soviet assault groups struck Kholm: the 1278th Rifle Regiment with tank support against Jagdkommando 8 in the south-west and the 82nd Rifle Regiment with tank support in the east against IR 386. The Soviet infantry were supported by a company of British-built Matilda II tanks, which proved nearly impervious to the German 3.7cm and 5cm PaK. Although the Jagdkommando repulsed the Soviet attack in their sector, IR 386's main defensive line was penetrated and the Soviet attack there made a large dent in Kholm's defensive perimeter. Scherer's headquarters came under direct fire and he was lightly wounded. Although Scherer pleaded for Luftwaffe close air support, he only received sporadic assistance from Uckermann's artillery outside the pocket. Sometimes German troops knocked out these tanks with Teller anti-tank mines, dropped onto them from second-storey windows, but on other occasions the tanks shot everything up in sight and then returned to their own lines once their

ammunition was expended. Soviet attacks continued near the break-in point for five more days, but IR 386 was finally able to seal off the breach. Kampfgruppe Scherer suffered over 550 casualties in this attack, lost two of four PaK guns and nearly exhausted its ammunition.

The nearest help for Scherer was located to the south-west, coming from the Loknya railway station, where the rest of Uckermann's 218. Infanterie-Division detrained. The OKH transferred XXXIX AK (mot.) under General der Panzertruppen Hans Jürgen von Arnim to AOK 16 to coordinate the relief of Kholm, but for the time being Arnim had less than a division under his control. Heeresgruppe Nord dispatched a reinforced *Kampfgruppe* from 8. Panzer-Division under Oberst Wilhelm Crissoli and most of Sturmgeschütz-Abteilung 184 to augment Arnim's tiny command. Kampfgruppe Crissoli, which had two infantry battalions from Schützen-Regiment 8, six tanks, artillery and engineers, was able to reach Dubrova, 9 miles (14.5km) south-west of Kholm, before it was stopped by Soviet blocking forces. With swamps and forests on both sides of the only road into Kholm, the Germans could not

easily bypass Soviet roadblocks. Purkaev was also able to get the fresh 45th Rifle Brigade to Kholm and Makarev deployed it on the west side of town to block Kampfgruppe Crissoli. Two T-34s were also placed in ambush on the west side of Kholm, knocking out a German tank and an assault gun. In heavy fighting on 31 January, Crissoli was badly wounded and Gruppe Uckermann was forced to shift to the defence. Uckermann received four battalions of Luftwaffe field troops and IR 553 from the 329. Infanterie-Division, but he knew that he lacked the strength to keep the road to Kholm open. Instead, Uckermann made the risky decision to bring most of his artillery as far forwards as possible to provide maximum firepower for Kampfgruppe Scherer and then had two artillery forward observers (FOs) flown into the city to direct the guns. In time, the two German FOs were able to call down heavy artillery fire within about 10 minutes, which Scherer used to break up Soviet attacks. However, by mid-February Makarev finally had enough artillery to neutralize the airfield, forcing Luftflotte I to begin using Go-242 gliders on 16 February. Hitler ordered one last attempt to use the airstrip on 25 February, but after four Ju-52s were lost to artillery fire, the airstrip was shut down. Kampfgruppe Scherer needed about 15 tons of ammunition and food a day to survive, which was met entirely by airdrop of 250kg *Mischlast Versorgungsbomben* (supply bombs) and glider deliveries. Scherer's men set up a landing zone on the frozen river Lovat, but many canisters fell behind Soviet lines. Furthermore, the Soviets set up anti-aircraft batteries to engage the slow-moving transports and gliders, which succeeded in inflicting painful losses, but the Germans responded by preceding airdrops with suppressive bombardments on the flak sites by Stukas and Gruppe Uckermann's artillery. Out of 81 gliders eventually dispatched to Kholm, 56 reached the garrison but Scherer's men were literally living hand to mouth.

Unable to break into the town, Makarev simply used his artillery to pulverize each major building in the town. With roofs blasted in, the German troops were denied shelter from the bitter -40° F (-40° C) cold, which eroded their health and morale. Over a thousand German wounded were sheltered in cellars in the ruins, with only two doctors and limited medical supplies. Kholm's civilians were also still in place, but with even fewer resources than Scherer's men. Amazingly, the heavy losses suffered by repeated Soviet attacks caused a number of Russian troops to defect to Scherer's garrison, where they were put to work as manual labour in constructing defences. However, the artillery bombardments were merely a prelude to the main event. The 3rd Shock Army had received the 2nd GRC and Purkaev intended to use it to resolve the situation at Kholm. On the morning of 21 February, Purkaev made his big push, beginning with an attack west of Kholm by the fresh 130th Rifle Division and 27th and 75th Rifle Brigades against Uckermann's artillery strongpoint near Dubrova. After a two-day battle, Dubrova was captured and Gruppe Uckermann forced to withdraw, which temporarily reduced the fire support available to Kholm. Meanwhile, the replenished 33rd and 391st Rifle Divisions attacked the south-east side of Kholm on 24 February, while the fresh 37th Rifle Brigade attacked the north side of the town – for the first time, Scherer was faced with simultaneous concentric attacks. Indeed, the Soviet attacks in late February were probably the most critical moment for

TOP
Kampfgruppe Scherer started out with only a single 50mm PaK 38 anti-tank gun inside Kholm and it had to keep moving it around to protect it from Soviet artillery fire. Here, the gun has been positioned behind ruins in the centre of town and camouflaged with white parachutes from supply drops. Eventually, Scherer received two more PaK 38s by air and incorporated two captured 45mm guns into his defence. (Author's collection)

BOTTOM
A T-60 light tank, burning on the outskirts of Kholm. The lightly armed and poorly protected T-60 was intended as a scout tank, not an urban assault vehicle, but the North-western Front was forced to use whatever tanks it had to reinforce its infantry assaults. Attacking in platoon-sized groups, Soviet tanks were easy targets for Scherer's *Panzerjäger*. (Author's collection)

A German soldier recovers a 250kg *Mischlast Versorgungsbombe* (mixed load, supply bomb) inside Kholm. These containers could be dropped fairly accurately and carried a mix of ammunition, food and medical supplies. However, the troops of the garrison were so exhausted by inadequate rations, lack of sleep and exposure to sub-zero temperatures that recovering a 250kg container in deep snow became a nearly superhuman task. (Author's collection)

Kampfgruppe Scherer during the entire siege. Yet somehow, Scherer's men held out and although Soviet tanks and infantry reached the GPU building, they could not capture it.

While Scherer's men hung on by their fingernails, living only from airdrop to airdrop, Arnim cobbled together a rescue force. Even by early March, XXXIX AK still had assembled fewer than two divisions, but Arnim decided to try and push through to Kholm. Just as the attack was beginning on 5 March, the freezing weather worsened and Soviet resistance stiffened. Arnim's forces had suffered over 5,000 casualties since mid-January and were too depleted to fight their way through 3rd Shock Army blocking units. Instead, he was forced to call off the attack and wait for better weather and to replenish his units.

Inside Kholm, the battle had devolved into a medieval siege, conducted with 20th-century weapons. Most of the horses had been eaten except for a few retained to pull guns around and the daily bread ration was down to 10½oz (300g). By the end of March, more than half of Kampfgruppe Scherer was either wounded or seriously ill, worsened by an outbreak of typhus. Scherer was forced to form reserve units from walking wounded and he barely had enough men standing to man the perimeter. Just when it seemed that it couldn't get any worse for the defenders, the spring thaw arrived in early April, melting the ice-walls, the drop zone on the Lovat and leaving much of the town in pools of melting snow. Without the cover afforded by ice-walls, the Soviets gained better observation into the town and their constant sniper and mortar fire made daylight movement difficult. The 3rd Shock Army kept up the pressure throughout April, launching repeated attacks between 2 and 18 April. In contrast to their normal poorly planned attacks, a carefully planned Soviet attack by a single rifle battalion, supported by three heavy tanks achieved a major success on 10 April and captured a large chunk of the northern section of town. The KV-1 tanks proved impervious to the German

PaK guns and were only stopped by the Policeman's Ravine, which they could not cross. Despite Scherer's pleading, Luftwaffe air support failed to intervene and Kampfgruppe Scherer suffered another 500 casualtties in this period. However, Purkaev was forced to divert a great deal of 3rd Shock Army's resources to continue pushing towards Velikiye Luki in the south-west and his forces at Kholm were insufficient to break Scherer's defence. Indeed, Scherer's skilful defence of Kholm was one of the great defensive actions in modern military history, ranking with Rorke's Drift.

THE GERMAN RELIEF OPERATIONS, MARCH–MAY 1942

Even though Kurochkin's troops had succeeded in surrounding II AK at Demyansk, by mid-March it was obvious that the North-western Front's Winter Counteroffensive had culminated. Despite pouring thousands of additional reinforcements into the battle, the Soviets had failed to capture Staraya Russa, Kholm or Demyansk. Owing to the fact that II AK still held the Knevitsy–Lychkovo stretch of the Staraya Russa–Valday railway line, 11th Army and 1st Shock Army continued to run their supply lines over icy marsh trails stretching back over 70 miles (110km) to Valday. The 3rd Shock Army was in slightly better shape, with a railhead at Ostashkov.

Kurochkin's troops were now paying for the inadequate logistic effort supporting the offensive. The front-line Soviet troops were semi-starved and short on ammunition – little better than the Germans inside the Demyansk pocket. Indeed, the Luftwaffe was winning the logistic battle hands down for the German Army, which was getting more food and ammunition than its opponents. Lacking the supplies to maintain the initiative, most Soviet front-line divisions slid into a siege mentality. Small-scale attacks continued all around the pocket, but without the strength needed to break the defence. Brockdorff-Ahlefeldt used the advantage of interior lines within the pocket to shuffle his small reserves around just in time to strengthen threatened sectors, while Kurochkin found it difficult to mass elements of four armies operating on exterior lines.

A German StuG III assault gun from Sturmgeschütz-Abteilung 184 enters Kholm on 5 May 1942, ending the 105-day siege of the city. (Author's collection)

Busch began preparing plans to relieve both Demyansk and Kholm in early March, but his forces were still barely able to hold their own, never mind go over to the offensive. Hitler had promised the transfer of five divisions to AOK 16 to relieve Demyansk, but as of 10 March only two complete divisions – 5. and 8. leichte Infanterie-Divisionen – had arrived. Parts of 122. Infanterie-Division (five infantry battalions) and 329. Infanterie-Division (five battalions) were also in the process of arriving by rail, but the rest of their divisions were not available. The OKH also provided Kampfgruppe Hoffman from 7. Gebirgs-Division (five battalions, four infantry and one artillery) as well as Luftwaffe-Division Meindl. Busch would have preferred to wait until the rest of these formations arrived, but Hitler demanded that the relief operation for Demyansk begin no later than 21 March. Busch also directed XXXIX AK to organize a smaller relief operation for Kholm, although the forces available for that effort barely amounted to a division. In addition, X AK still had to devote considerable effort to holding Staraya Russa with 18. and 81. Infanterie-Divisionen.

Hansen picked Seydlitz to lead Operation *Brückenschlag* (*Bridge Building*), the operation to relieve Demyansk. Seydlitz decided to make 5. and 8. leichte Infanterie-Divisionen his main effort in the centre, to advance 14 miles (22km) from the Staraya Russa–Kholm road to the Lovat River at Ramushevo, where they would be met by Korpsgruppe Zorn attacking out of the pocket. Many of the infantry units coming from Germany had been so hastily assembled that they were not even fully equipped, and X AK provided Seydlitz with 90 captured British Vickers and 30 Russian Maxim machine guns, as well as some Russian 45mm anti-tank guns. Busch provided Seydlitz 30 tanks from I/Panzer-Regiment 203 and 13 StuG IIIs from two different assault gun units. On paper, Korpsgruppe Seydlitz had about 150 medium artillery pieces in support, although few batteries had arrived at the front when the offensive began. Far more important for Seydlitz was the amount of engineer and air support available. Although temperatures still hovered around -13 to 20° F (-20 to -6° C), the spring thaw was not far away and he knew that pioneers would be required to bridge the numerous water obstacles in the area and to clear forest tracks. Luftwaffe close air support would be critical for maintaining attack momentum and reducing Soviet strongpoints.

Seydlitz kicked off *Brückenschlag* at 0730hrs on 21 March, with three battalions of 8. leichte Infanterie-Division and two battalions of 5. leichte Infanterie-Division, plus some armour, advancing about 540yd (500m) eastwards through forest land towards the river Red'ya. Infanterie-Regiment 51 from 18. Infanterie-Division (mot.) recaptured Penno, to protect the northern flank of Seydlitz's assault group. Soviet resistance, primarily from 254th Rifle Division, was stiff despite Stuka attacks. Kurochkin had expected a relief attempt by X AK after the Demyansk pocket was created and he put his chief of staff, General-Lieutenant Nikolai Vatutin, in charge of establishing an outer ring around the pocket and Vatutin had just established a defence in depth before Seydlitz struck. The two German light divisions advanced slowly and methodically, in temperatures of -4° F (-20° C), but their southern flank grew increasingly long and exposed. Seydlitz was forced to redirect 122. and 329. Infanterie-Divisionen to protect his southern flank, capturing the towns of Sokolovo and Ozhedovo, but reducing the forces pushing towards Ramushevo. After two days of fighting, 8. leichte Infanterie-Division reached the river Red'ya at Kudrovo, but Korpsgruppe Seydlitz was not across in force until 27 March. Morozov had husbanded his reserve, the 20 T-34 tanks of 69th Tank Brigade, which he now hurled into the flank of 5. Jäger-Division. In a desperate battle near Jaswy, the *Jäger* destroyed eight T-34s and repulsed Morozov's counterattack, but Seydlitz's advance was temporarily brought to a halt. By the end of March, Seydlitz was still 4½ miles (7km) from Ramushevo and 12½ miles (20km) from Kampfgruppe Eicke inside the pocket.

In early April, the weather began to break and the spring thaw reduced the land to a quagmire. German supply trucks had to move through axle-deep mud, while horses pulling artillery pieces became mired and many broke their legs. Seydlitz ordered his pioneers to build corduroy roads through the marshes with fallen trees, but the German advance was reduced to a crawl. It was not until 12 April that the troops of Gebirgsjäger-Regiment 206 first saw the town of Ramushevo in the distance. Two days later, Korpsgruppe Zorn began Operation *Fallreep* (*Gangway*) at 1100hrs on 14 April. Zorn

During the summer of 1942, the Germans used Soviet POWs and civilians to build a narrow-gauge railway line from Staraya Russa into the neck of the Ramushevo corridor. This railway line was under constant attack by Soviet artillery. (Author's collection)

Operation *Brückenschlag*, 21 March to 21 April 1942

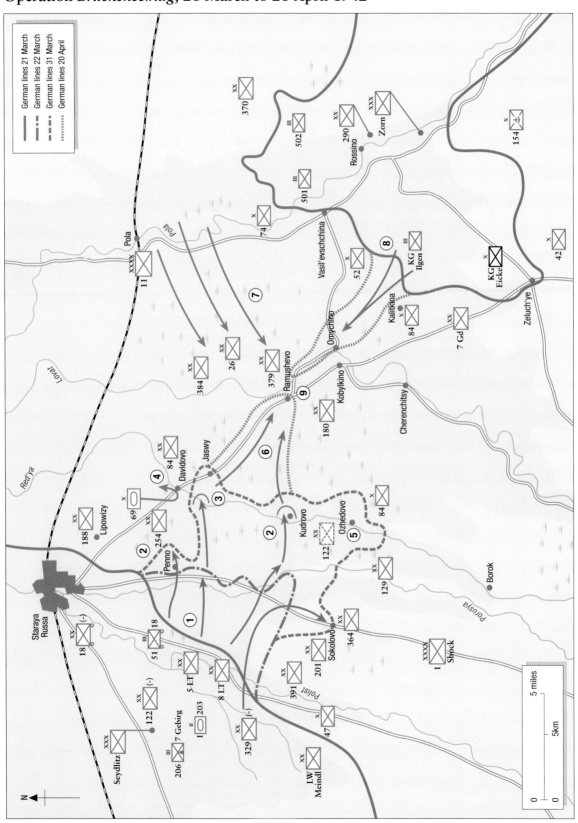

had formed an assault regiment with five battalions from 32. Infanterie-Division and a mixed battalion from the rest of II AK and he used it to batter a thin wedge through 7th Guards Rifle Division towards the Lovat. It still took another week of fighting for Seydlitz's troops to capture Ramushevo and for Zorn to clear the opposite river bank. At 1830hrs on 21 April, the first pioneers from Korpsgruppe Seydlitz crossed the Lovat River in assault boats and linked up with Eicke's Waffen-SS men. A tenuous ground link, less than 2½ miles (4km) wide was soon established and German pioneers began sending supply barges across the Lovat River on 22 April. The Demyansk pocket had been relieved, although the ordeal for II AK was far from over. Operation *Brückenschlag* had cost X AK over 10,000 casualties and, since the beginning of the Soviet Winter Counteroffensive, II and X AK had suffered 63,000 casualties, including 17,000 dead or missing. On the Soviet side, the North-western Front's Winter Counteroffensive had cost Kurochkin's forces over 245,000 casualties, including 88,908 dead or missing.

Further south, XXXIX AK made another effort to relieve Kholm with Operation *Grün* at the end of April. The assault group was formed under Generalleutnant Viktor Lang, who had replaced a seriously ill Uckermann, and composed the bulk of 218. Infanterie-Division, IR 411 from 122. Infanterie-Division, 20 tanks from 8. Panzer-Division and a dozen assault guns from Sturmgeschütz-Abteilung 184. An accompanying *Panzerjäger* battalion from 8. Panzer-Division was also given an unusually large number of 5cm PaK 38 anti-tank guns in an effort to counter the T-34 tanks blocking the road into Kholm. The attack up the road to Kholm began on 30 April and Gruppe Lang had to fight its way past the tough 8th Guards Rifle Division. Purkaev also committed part of 71st Tank Brigade to block the road into Kholm. German progress up the road was slow, but steady as Luftwaffe support blasted one Soviet position after another.

Once it became apparent that Gruppe Lang might actually reach Kholm, Purkaev decided to make one last grand play to seize the town. On the night of 30 April to 1 May, the Soviet artillery began the heaviest bombardment yet of Kholm. Many of Scherer's heavy weapons were put out of action. Then at 0545hrs on 1 May, three rifle regiments and 15 tanks from 3rd Shock Army launched a powerful concentric attack against the defenders. Soviet tanks broke into the town and Scherer's defence around the 'Red Ruin' in the eastern part of town was on the verge of collapse. Scherer called quickly for Stuka support, which helped to break up the Soviet attack momentum. A new 5cm PaK 38 gun was also flown in by glider to augment his anti-tank defence, since several guns had been put out of action. Seven Soviet tanks were destroyed near the airstrip. Heavy fighting continued in Kholm for the next seven hours and it was not until the afternoon that the Soviet attacks were contained. On the night of 4 May, Gruppe Lang was almost within sight of Kholm and Arnim ordered a night attack to breach the last Soviet defences.

1 21 March, Gruppe Seydlitz begins relief operation with advance to Porusya River led by 5. and 8. leichte Infanterie-Divisionen.

2 23 March, IR 51 captures Penno and 8. leichte Infanterie-Division secures crossing over Red'ya at Kudrovo.

3 25 March, 5. leichte Infanterie-Division captures Jaswy on Staraya Russa–Ramushevo road.

4 27 March, counterattack by 69th Tank Brigade with 20 T-34 tanks into flank of 5. leichte Infanterie-Division near Jaswy.

5 29 March, 122. Infanterie-Division seizes Ozhedovo.

6 12 April, Gebirgsjäger-Regiment 206 leads the breakthrough towards Ramushevo.

7 11th Army transfers three rifle divisions to Lovat River area to prevent Seydlitz from breaking through.

8 14 April, Korpsgruppe Zorn begins *Fallreep*, with Kampfgruppe Ilgen attacking towards Omychino.

9 21 April, Seydlitz's troops establish tenuous link with KG Ilgen at Ramushevo.

Soviet engineers assist a truck in negotiating its way across a flimsy wooden bridge. The primary weakness of the North-western Front was logistics. Attacking through marshes and thick forests caught AOK 16 by surprise in January 1942 but once the spring thaw arrived, the North-western Front faced great difficulty resupplying its front-line troops. (Phil Curme)

After heavy fighting and with Stukas in direct support, IR 411 broke through the final 3rd Shock Army positions and a small detachment with two assault guns and 60 troops was sent ahead to link up with Kampfgruppe Scherer around 0620hrs on 5 May. By the time that Kampfgruppe Scherer was relieved after its 105-day siege in Kholm, the garrison had suffered 60 per cent casualties with over 1,500 killed and 2,200 wounded from an original force of around 4,500 troops. The unsuccessful siege of Kholm cost Purkaev's 3rd Shock Army about 20,000–25,000 casualties. After Kholm was relieved, 218. Infanterie-Division moved into the town, which was integrated into the German front line, while Scherer's survivors were given generous home leave in Germany. Kholm remained in German hands until February 1944.

THE BATTLE OF THE RAMUSHEVO CORRIDOR, MAY–OCTOBER 1942

Kurochkin's forces were too fought-out to react immediately to the German creation of the land bridge to Demyansk, but the Stavka was soon on his back to sever this tenuous link and then proceed with crushing the pocket. Stung by this setback, the Stavka provided Kurochkin with nine artillery regiments from the RGVK reserve to augment his meagre firepower and he planned to focus it on crushing the German units in the Ramushevo corridor. Group Ksenofontov was permanently detached from the Kalinin Front, redesignated as 53rd Army and assigned to contain the southern side of the Demyansk pocket. On 3 May, 11th Army attacked the north side of the corridor while 1st Shock Army attacked the south side. The Soviet troops continued to attack for two weeks, but could not cut the 2½-mile-wide (4km) corridor, although artillery fire prevented the German supply convoys from using the road most of the time. Consequently, II AK was still forced to rely heavily upon the Luftwaffe for its supplies, even after the creation of the land bridge. Not only was the May offensive a failure but from 7–11 June 1st Shock Army's 1st GRC was obliged to withdraw from a vulnerable salient on the south side of the corridor.

After the Soviet offensive concluded, II AK took time to improve its defences, replenish its depleted ranks and deal with the local partisans and civilian population. Although II AK relied upon local civilians to harvest crops within the Demyansk salient, it also recognized the connection between the civilians and Vasilyev's partisans. On 26 May, Brockdorff-Ahlefeldt issued an order to deport all non-vital Russians to the Reich as forced labour. Thousands of Russian civilians were deported from within the Demyansk salient throughout the summer of 1942, which helped to reduce the demand for food and to deny support to Vasilyev's partisans. By late 1942, partisan activity around Demyansk had dwindled to almost nothing. AOK 16 also used the interregnum between Soviet attacks to build a narrow-gauge railway (*Feldeisenbahn*) from Staraya Russa down to the Pola River, to improve its logistic capability into the corridor but owing to Soviet artillery harassment, the railway line could not be extended all the way to Demyansk. Korpsgruppe Zorn – now under General der Panzertruppen Otto von Knobelsdorff – was tasked with defending the corridor. German pioneers quickly turned the area into a fortified zone, complete with deep barbed wire obstacles and liberally seeded with S- and Teller mines. In the sector held by 123. Infanterie-Division, German engineers emplaced 22,000 mines and 400 rolls of barbed wire. Local civilians were forced to repair the Staraya Russa–Demyansk road and to build new bunkers and artillery-proof shelters for German troops. After the destruction of 2nd Shock Army in the swamps of the Volkhov, AOK 18 was able to transfer 126. Infanterie-Division to reinforce Korpsgruppe Knobelsdorff. AOK 16 also received a batch of 75mm PaK 40 anti-tank guns and Knobelsdorff was able to mass over 200 anti-tank guns in the Ramushevo corridor.

Pausing to regroup after the failed May offensive, Kurochkin was given much of June to rebuild his forces and prepare for a deliberate offensive in July. The North-western Front now comprised five armies (1st Shock, 11th, 27th, 34th and 53rd) with over 300,000 combat troops in 29 divisions, plus 6th Air Army. Kurochkin shifted General-Major Fedor P. Ozerov's 27th Army to hold the front against Staraya Russa, while concentrating Morozov's 11th Army on the north side of the Ramushevo corridor. Similarly, 1st Shock Army was concentrated on the south side of the corridor, while 34th and 53rd Armies held the remainder of the ring around Demyansk. The Stavka provided Kurochkin with considerably more artillery and tanks than he had for the Winter Counteroffensive, although logistic support was still inadequate.

Kurochkin began his second attempt to sever the Ramushevo corridor at 1400hrs on 17 July. He used his new artillery firepower to deliver a 90-minute bombardment, then launched a concentric attack by 11th Army and 1st Shock Army's 1st GRC. However, the Soviet bombardment barely scratched the German defences and the Soviet infantry and tanks attacked straight into carefully prepared engagement areas which quickly ground up the shock groups. Soviet artillery ammunition stocks were insufficient to support a protracted battle and the attack quickly degenerated into a World War I-style battle of attrition that favoured the defenders. After a week of futile attacks, the Soviet offensive collapsed after gaining less than a mile of terrain. Kurochkin's stock fell rapidly after this offensive and Stalin was infuriated that the North-western Front seemed incapable of severing the Ramushevo corridor.

On 2 August, the Stavka sent a directive to Kurochkin informing him that Marshal Semen Timoshenko was being sent to help plan and supervise the next offensive, but it was clear that he was intended as a replacement.

BATTLE FOR THE RAMUSHEVO CORRIDOR, 17 JULY 1942 (pp. 78–79)

After the Germans managed to reopen a land corridor to Demyansk in April 1942, the Stavka wasted little time in ordering the North-western Front to sever it in order to isolate the German II AK. Kurochkin launched four major offensives between May and September, each relying upon greater and greater doses of firepower rather than manoeuvre to accomplish his objective. Since the corridor was only 4 miles (6km) wide, it seemed that attacking it from both sides simultaneously would succeed. Unfortunately, the Germans had just enough time to heavily reinforce and fortified this narrow corridor and each Soviet offensive was bloodily repulsed.

One of the strongest attacks came at the village of Vasil'evschchina **(1)** on the northern side of the corridor on 17 July 1942, where the 11th Army tried to batter its way through the 8. Jäger-Division's main line of resistance. After a 90-minute artillery preparation, two Soviet rifle divisions **(2)** attacked the positions of Jäger-Regiment 38 at 1530hrs. During the winter battles, Kurochkin had only limited artillery, tank and air support available, which made fortified German *Stutzpünkt* a very difficult nut to crack. However during the July offensive, 11th Army finally had significant fire support available and the

Stutzpünkt proved very vulnerable to artillery bombardment and attack by Il-2 Sturmovik ground-support aircraft **(3)**. Although the attackers lost tanks and infantry getting through the German minefields, the German defences had been sufficiently softened up that the Soviet infantry and tanks swarmed over the position and were able to capture Vasil'evschchina. From this position, the 11th Army could push south-east 6 miles (10km) to Loznitsy, severing II AK's only supply route.

Surprised by the sudden loss of the critical *Stutzpünkt* at Vasil'evschchina, 8. Jäger-Division ordered Jäger-Regiment 38 to counterattack immediately. Amazingly, the *Jäger* not only recovered the village, but succeeded in pushing the Soviet assault groups back in disarray. The Soviets continued to attack in this sector for the next six days and gradually ground JR 38 into dust; its first and second battalions could barely field 100 men altogether by the end of the battle. Overall, 8. Jäger-Division suffered over 1,500 casualties in a week. Yet by the time that Kurochkin was eventually forced to admit failure and suspend the offensive, there were 59 knocked-out Soviet tanks and thousands of dead around the obscure village of Vasil'evschchina.

The directive stated that, 'the Stavka considers this plan [Kurochkin's] a mess, since the front and you, in particular, cannot fulfil it'. It also stated that, 'Marshal Timoshenko has been given the authority to give you orders and alter your dispositions if they turn out to be pointless, and to replace people if they turn out to be unfit to fulfil the assigned missions'. There was little doubt now that Kurochkin's future was in jeopardy, which made his next plan a conservative repeat of the last one. Nor would Timoshenko's presence make any difference, since he had no talent for detailed planning and was little more than a figurehead. The main problem for Kurochkin was that he could not employ deceptive *maskirova* – and was thereby denied the advantage of surprise – since the Stavka condemned him to keep attacking the Ramushevo corridor. Given the fact that AOK 16 had 13 of its 16 divisions tied up defending the Demyansk salient or protecting the Ramushevo corridor, an attack elsewhere would have had greater probability of success and drawn forces away from the corridor, but Kurochkin was constrained to do as directed by Timoshenko and the Stavka.

The only real difference between the Soviet August offensive and its predecessors was that the Stavka directed Kurochkin to conduct local attacks with 27th, 34th and 53rd Armies around the periphery of the Demyansk salient. These attacks were easily fended off by the well-fortified II AK, but they reduced the amount of logistic support available for the main effort. When the offensive began on 10 August, there was enough artillery ammunition for only a 10-minute bombardment, which failed to dent Korpsgruppe Knobelsdorff's defences. The 11th Army attacked from the north with six rifle divisions and over 100 tanks, while 1st Shock Army attacked from the south with three rifle divisions and 30 tanks. The Germans literally shot the Soviet shock groups to pieces in their obstacle belts and even after a week of fighting the Soviets failed to penetrate more than a few hundred metres into the German defences. German minefields inflicted horrendous casualties, including General-Major Nikanor D. Zakhvataev, commander of 1st GRC. By 21 August, Kurochkin was forced to halt the offensive because of heavy casualties and insufficient ammunition. As before, the Soviets were able to bring the Staraya Russa–Demyansk road under artillery fire, but they could not break through the German fortified zone in the corridor. The August offensive had been a disaster for the North-western Front and the only thing worse would be to repeat the mistake, which was exactly what the Stavka told Kurochkin to do.

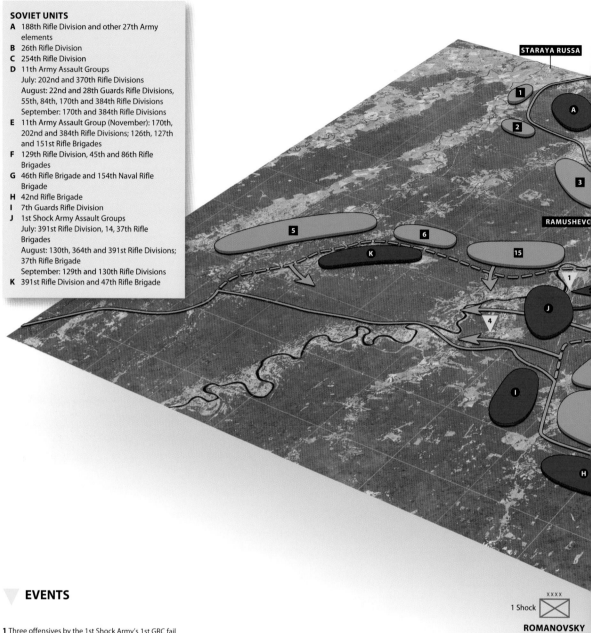

STARAYA RUSSA

SOVIET UNITS

A 188th Rifle Division and other 27th Army elements
B 26th Rifle Division
C 254th Rifle Division
D 11th Army Assault Groups
  July: 202nd and 370th Rifle Divisions
  August: 22nd and 28th Guards Rifle Divisions, 55th, 84th, 170th and 384th Rifle Divisions
  September: 170th and 384th Rifle Divisions
E 11th Army Assault Group (November): 170th, 202nd and 384th Rifle Divisions; 126th, 127th and 151st Rifle Brigades
F 129th Rifle Division, 45th and 86th Rifle Brigades
G 46th Rifle Brigade and 154th Naval Rifle Brigade
H 42nd Rifle Brigade
I 7th Guards Rifle Division
J 1st Shock Army Assault Groups
  July: 391st Rifle Division, 14, 37th Rifle Brigades
  August: 130th, 364th and 391st Rifle Divisions; 37th Rifle Brigade
  September: 129th and 130th Rifle Divisions
K 391st Rifle Division and 47th Rifle Brigade

RAMUSHEVO

1 Shock
ROMANOVSKY

▼ EVENTS

1 Three offensives by the 1st Shock Army's 1st GRC fail in July, August and September.

2 All three offensives by 11th Army in July, August and September fail as well.

3 By the end of summer, 126. Infanterie-Division takes over more of southern sector, releasing SS-'Totenkopf' to shift position.

4 September–October, Operation *Michael* mauls 1st GRC and widens the southern side of the corridor.

5 Timoshenko shifts axis for his November offensive, which captures Pustynya, but fails to achieve a breakthrough.

THE BATTLE OF THE RAMUSHEVO CORRIDOR, JULY–NOVEMBER 1942

The Germans manage to hold open the vital corridor to Demyansk despite repeated Soviet assaults.

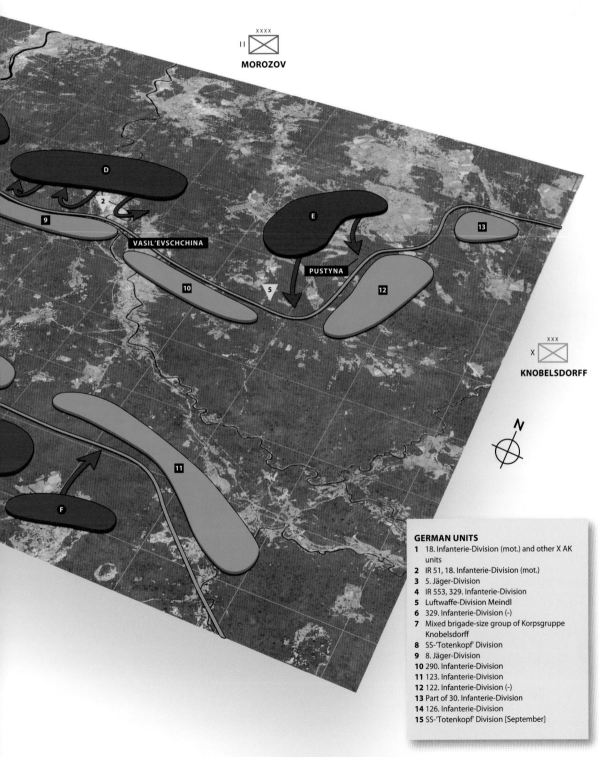

Note: Gridlines are shown at intervals of 5 km/3.10 miles

MOROZOV

VASIL'EVSCHCHINA

PUSTYNA

KNOBELSDORFF

N

GERMAN UNITS
1 18. Infanterie-Division (mot.) and other X AK units
2 IR 51, 18. Infanterie-Division (mot.)
3 5. Jäger-Division
4 IR 553, 329. Infanterie-Division
5 Luftwaffe-Division Meindl
6 329. Infanterie-Division (-)
7 Mixed brigade-size group of Korpsgruppe Knobelsdorff
8 SS-'Totenkopf' Division
9 8. Jäger-Division
10 290. Infanterie-Division
11 123. Infanterie-Division
12 122. Infanterie-Division (-)
13 Part of 30. Infanterie-Division
14 126. Infanterie-Division
15 SS-'Totenkopf' Division [September]

After restocking his artillery, Kurochkin conducted a 90-minute bombardment on the Ramushevo corridor on 15 September, followed by a renewed ground assault by 11th Army and 1st Shock Army. Once again, the Soviet infantry shock groups failed to penetrate the German defences and were shot to pieces. The North-western Front's front-line armies were now thoroughly spent and demoralized by heavy losses. Furthermore, 1st GRC was itself forced to hold an exposed salient on the south side of the corridor. Busch had been waiting for the Soviets to exhaust themselves against his prepared defences and now he saw his chance to deliver a powerful riposte while they were still off balance. While AOK 16 lacked the strength to widen the Ramushevo corridor during the summer of 1942, it now had an opportunity to crush the troublesome 1st GRC. Busch placed 5. Jäger-Division and 126. Infanterie-Division, I/Panzer-Regiment 203 and Sturmgeschütz-Abteilung 184 under Korpsgruppe Knobelsdorff for Operation *Michael*.

Operation *Michael* began on 27 September with an attack by 5. Jäger-Division and 126. Infanterie Division on the east side of 1st GRC's salient, against 7th Guards Rifle Division. Supported by Luftwaffe ground attack aircraft and a 50-minute artillery preparation, the Germans were able to surround and overwhelm one of 7th GRD's rifle regiments within a matter of hours. Kurochkin rushed three more rifle divisions to reinforce the overextended 1st Shock Army, but the Germans methodically defeated these units as they arrived piecemeal. Owing to the weakness of 6th Air Army – reduced to only 35 operational fighters after months of continuous operations – the Luftwaffe was able to regain air superiority over the Ramushevo corridor and use its Stukas to support the ground offensive. After a six-day fight, the Germans smashed in the eastern side of the Soviet salient. Pausing briefly to re-organize, the Germans then struck the west side of the salient on 7 October with Division Meindl and part of SS-'Totenkopf'. With 1st Shock Army on the verge of a crushing defeat, Kurochkin finally accepted that he had to evacuate the salient. Encouraged by the success of *Michael*, AOK 16 decided to make one last effort before the winter arrived to expand the northern side of the Ramushevo corridor with Operation *Pußta* on 26–27 October. Yet despite committing elements of seven German divisions to the effort, *Pußta* failed to regain any ground and was called off after just two days.

LEFT

A Soviet 152mm ML-20 howitzer in firing position, June 1942. The Stavka continued to provide Kurochkin with greater amounts of artillery during the summer battles for the Ramushevo corridor, but Soviet assault groups still could not breach the German main lines of resistance. (RIA Novosti, 602487)

RIGHT

Soviet troops manhandle a 45mm anti-tank gun through a marshy area near Lake Il'men in July 1942. Even during summer months, off-road mobility was still restricted in this waterlogged terrain. (RIA Novosti, 212)

The German forces in the Demyansk salient went through a number of changes after the end of *Michael* and *Pußta*. After a year of continuous fighting around Demyansk, the exhausted SS-'Totenkopf' Division was transferred to France. Brockdorff-Ahlefeldt was also exhausted and seriously ill; he handed over command of II AK to General der Infanterie Paul Laux from 32. Infanterie-Division on 28 November and returned to Berlin. Laux, who had commanded the special *Korpsgruppe* defending the Ramushevo corridor, put Generalleutnant Gustav Höhne from 8. Jäger-Division in charge of the corridor.

Despite three major offensives against the Ramushevo corridor between July and September 1942, the North-western Front had failed to crack the German defences and had suffered another 300,000 casualties (including 90,000 dead). German casualties were about 72,000, including 16,000 dead. While AOK 16 had been bloodied by the incessant Soviet attacks, II AK still stood defiant within the Demyansk salient.

THE END GAME, NOVEMBER 1942 TO FEBRUARY 1943

Disgusted with Kurochkin's inability to sever the Ramushevo corridor, Stalin ordered Timoshenko to take command of the North-western Front on 17 November. Kurochkin was demoted to command 11th Army. Simultaneously, Morozov was shifted from command of 11th Army to 1st Shock Army. Timoshenko was directed by the Stavka to prepare for another offensive against the corridor, in conjunction with Marshal Zhukov's Operation *Mars* offensive against the Rzhev salient. Furthermore, Operation *Uranus* was about to begin at Stalingrad and the Stavka believed that continued attacks by North-western Front would help fix the OKH's attention on Demyansk. However, the Stavka continued to short-change the North-western Front in terms of combat logistics; Timoshenko's front-line troops were given only one basic load of ammunition and two to four days of rations.

Rather than continue attacking the heavily defended narrow neck of the Ramushevo corridor, Timoshenko decided to shift the next offensive farther eastwards, hoping that the German defences there would be less formidable. As a preliminary operation, Kurochkin's 11th Army conducted a division-sized night attack against Stützpunkt Pustynya on 23–24 November. The German 122. Infanterie-Division put up a tough fight against 202nd Rifle Division, but Pustynya finally fell on 26 November. Although Timoshenko had eliminated a troublesome German strongpoint, he had also alerted Busch that the North-western Front had shifted its main attack axis eastwards. On the morning of 28 November, Timoshenko began his main attack; 11th Army committed two rifle divisions, three rifle brigades and a tank brigade in the north, while 1st Shock Army attacked with one rifle division and two rifle brigades in the south. In the path of the Soviet onslaught, Gruppe Höhne had 8. Jäger-Division, 122. and 290. Infanterie-Divisionen on the northern side of the corridor and 126. Infanterie-Division on the southern side. While the Soviets enjoyed a 3:1 superiority in manpower in their attack sectors, the alerted German defenders decimated the Soviet shock groups while they were struggling through minefields and barbed wire obstacles. Dozens of Soviet T-34 tanks were knocked out by German *Panzerjäger*, who finally had enough anti-tank guns to defeat armoured attacks. Neither Soviet army made more than minor gains. Nevertheless, the Stavka – and particularly Zhukov, whose

The evacuation of the Demyansk salient, February 1943

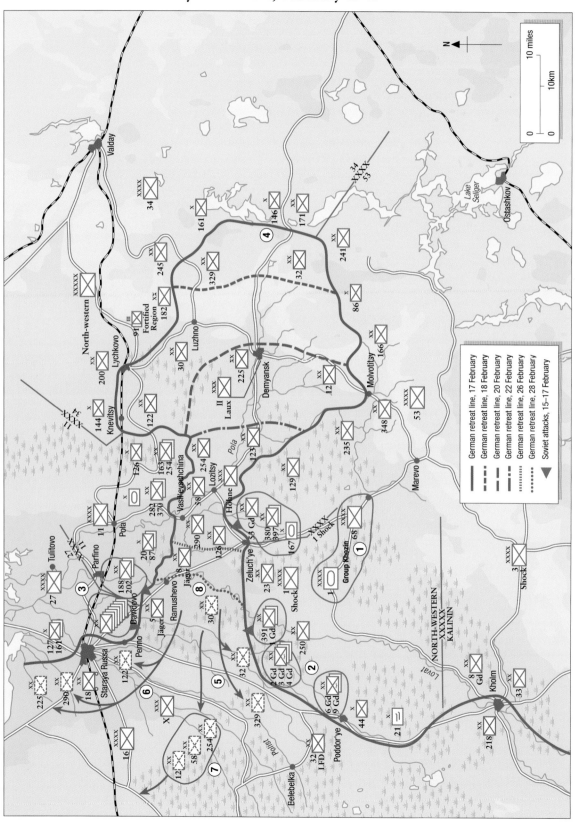

own *Mars* offensive was failing spectacularly – ordered Timoshenko to continue attacking after a brief pause to regroup. Generalfeldmarschall Georg von Küchler, commander of Heeresgruppe Nord, decided to reinforce Busch's hard-hit AOK 16 by transferring 58., 225. and 254. Infanterie-Divisionen from AOK 18's siege lines around Leningrad in order to reinforce the Ramushevo corridor.

Throughout December, Timoshenko's armies continued to jab at the German defences but the addition of three more German divisions to Gruppe Höhne resulted in each attack being repulsed with heavy losses. Despite a huge superiority in armour, the Soviets lost a total of 423 tanks over six weeks in trying to breach the German defences. Even worse, the Soviets had fallen into predictable habits which the Germans could exploit, such as attacking at the same time each day. When 1st Shock Army was spotted massing for another assault on 27 December, AOK 16 made a spoiling attack with ten artillery battalions that fired over 14,000 shells at Morozov's troops. The effects were devastating and 1st Shock Army was temporarily combat ineffective. Yet the Stavka ignored Timoshenko's requests to suspend the offensive and ordered him to continue with whatever forces were at hand. Just after New Year, a shock ground from 1st Shock Army consisting of 129th and 397th Rifle Divisions plus 177th Tank Brigade succeeded in making a penetration near Tsemena. However, II AK immediately counterattacked and surrounded the bulk of this force and then slowly annihilated it over the next two weeks. By the time that the Stavka finally allowed Timoshenko to suspend the offensive in early January 1943, most of the North-western Front's best divisions were battered wrecks.

While it was apparent that AOK 16's defences in the Demyansk salient were still formidable, the encirclement of the German AOK 6 at Stalingrad changed everything. The Wehrmacht was facing a catastrophe and needed every Luftwaffe transport plane to keep AOK 6 alive until a relief operation could be mounted and fresh divisions to restore the shattered southern front. At a stroke, Demyansk had been transformed from a fortress into an expensive liability. Generaloberst Kurt Zeitzler, the new head of the OKH had been working on Hitler for weeks, trying to convince him to abandon the Demyansk and Rzhev salients, but it was not until it became obvious that AOK 6 was about to be annihilated that Hitler began to listen. Finally, on 31 January Hitler authorized Zeitzler to evacuate the Demyansk and Rzhev salients and Busch was informed the next day. Hitler demanded that AOK 16 conduct a scorched earth policy in the Demyansk salient, destroying anything of use to the Red Army. The OKH stipulated that the evacuation would be completed within 70 days. Busch's staff had already been quietly preparing plans for evacuation and these were now stepped up.

While the Germans were preparing to evacuate the Demyansk salient, Timoshenko was preparing for another go at the Ramushevo corridor. After

1 The North-western Front forms an exploitation force, Group Khozin, composed of 1st Tank Army and 68th Army.

2 The Stavka provides five Guards Airborne Divisions to 1st Shock Army to attack 21. Luftwaffe-Feld-Division.

3 Between Penno and Ramushevo, 27th Army and 11th Army mass nine rifle divisions and 150 tanks against 5. Jäger-Division.

4 Operation *Ziethen* begins with 32. and 329. Infanterie-Divisionen evacuating the eastern end of the salient on 17 February.

5 The 32. and 329. Infanterie-Divisionen are immediately sent to reinforce the vulnerable sector opposite 1st Shock Army.

6 As the evacuation of the salient continues, 122., 225. and 290. Infanterie-Divisionen are sent to reinforce the sector around Staraya Russa and Lake Il'men.

7 Three divisions evacuated from the salient are transferred to AOK 18 on the Volkhov front.

8 The German evacuation stops on the Lovat River, where a fortified zone has been created on the west bank.

the failure of his Operation *Mars* at Rzhev, Zhukov proposed a new multi-front offensive known as *Polar Star* to be conducted by the Volkhov and North-western Fronts finally to crush the Demyansk salient and then roll up the right flank of AOK 16. Zhukov confidently expected that once II AK was eliminated, *Polar Star* would pave the way for the relief of Leningrad. Accepting Zhukov's concept for *Polar Star*, the Stavka provided Timoshenko with a mass of reinforcements, including the newly created 1st Tank Army and 68th Army, as well as five Guards Airborne Divisions. He placed 1st Tank and 68th Army in the newly formed Group Khozin in order to conduct a deep operation north-west towards Luga. Timoshenko planned to attack the northern side of the Ramushevo corridor with 27th and 11th Armies, the southern side of the corridor with 1st Shock Army, 53rd Army and the airborne divisions. Zhukov was confident that Gruppe Höhne could not withstand simultaneous attack by four Soviet armies. However, Soviet logistics were still in a mess, with front-line units dependent upon railheads that were still 40–60 miles (60–100km) distant. Consequently, it took longer to reposition units than expected and ammunition was in short supply. Timoshenko began to receive intelligence reports about unusual activity in the Demyansk salient and he was uncertain if the Germans were sending in more reinforcements or evacuating. Prodded by Zhukov, Timoshenko decided to attack immediately on the morning of 15 February 1943 with 11th and 53rd Armies, even though 1st Shock and 27th Armies still needed another week to redeploy. Predictably, the poorly prepared piecemeal Soviet attacks were repulsed with heavy losses. Without a breakthrough, Group Khozin could not be committed and *Polar Star* collapsed.

Soviet infantry from 11th Army attacking towards the Ramushevo corridor, summer 1942. Few Soviet attacks in mid-1942 were this organized, with smoke and heavy machine guns overlooking infantry. Too often, Soviet attacks were rushed affairs designed to satisfy demands from the Stavka (and Stalin) for progress. (RIA Novosti, 618709)

As the autumn of 1942 arrived, AOK 16 was still defending the Ramushevo corridor. Here, a battalion command post occupies a dugout. Note the hollow-charge anti-tank magnetic mines on the right. (Ian Barter)

Despite another defensive success, it was clear that AOK 16 could not expect any more reinforcements and that Timoshenko would continue to attack the corridor. General Laux, the new commander of II AK, requested permission to begin the evacuation sooner than anticipated and Busch agreed. On the morning of 17 February, II AK initiated Operation *Ziethen*, a phased withdrawal from the Demyansk salient. Beginning from the easternmost tip of the salient with 32. and 329. Infanterie-Divisionen, the German II AK began a series of retrograde movements, pulling its units back to successive resistance lines. As they withdrew, German troops burned villages and destroyed bridges to slow the Soviet pursuit. Most remaining Russian civilians were also taken by force and farm animals slaughtered. Owing to the scorched earth activity, the Soviets quickly detected the evacuation and Zhukov demanded that Timoshenko begin an immediate pursuit. Soviet ski troops were committed from 34th and 53rd Armies and while they did harass the retreating German units, they were unable to inflict any serious harm. The II AK continued to evacuate the salient, abandoning Demyansk – which was burnt to the ground – on 21 February. Five days later, the Germans had abandoned most of the Ramushevo corridor and by early March they withdrew to prepared defensive positions on the west bank of the Lovat River. Timoshenko's forces followed sullenly, unable to catch the retreating Germans. By the time that the final Soviet offensive ended, the North-western Front had suffered more than 33,000 casualties, including 10,000 dead. After 13 months of fighting, one of the longest battles on the Eastern Front had ended, but who was the victor?

AFTERMATH

Hitler wasted little time, believing that Demyansk was a defensive success for the Wehrmacht and he sought to commemorate the achievement with the Demyansk Shield, which was issued to all survivors of the campaign beginning in April 1943. German morale needed a shot in the arm after the Stalingrad debacle and Hitler believed that singling out Kholm and Demyansk would help. AOK 16 had built an impregnable fortified zone in the Ramushevo corridor which no Soviet attack ever broke – a rarity on the Eastern Front. The Demyansk campaign had tied up five Soviet armies against only a single German army for more than a year and had inflicted heavy and disproportionate losses upon the Red Army. Although exact figures are uncertain, the North-western Front suffered in excess of 600,000 casualties during the Demyansk campaign, including 200,000 dead. In return, AOK 16 suffered 188,000 casualties, including 48,000 dead or missing. Put in perspective, the North-western Front suffered nearly twice the losses that the British Army incurred in the battle of Passchendaele in 1917 and yet gained far less ground. To Hitler, who had been at Passchendaele, Demyansk and Kholm seemed like triumphs of the German warrior spirit.

A big part of the German success at Demyansk was based on logistic effort. Not only had the Luftwaffe committed a major part of its transport force to sustain II AK, but AOK 16 invested the effort throughout 1942 to build roads and bridges that enabled it to fight a protracted battle of attrition in the Ramushevo corridor. The Soviets did not and by autumn 1942, II AK was firing three times as much artillery ammunition as the North-western Front, which enabled the Germans to smother each attack. Yet holding onto Demyansk and Kholm required the commitment of 14 divisions and the bulk of the Luftwaffe transport assets in Russia. The diversion of so many divisions to hold and relieve useless positions such as Demyansk served to deprive the Wehrmacht of any kind of strategic reserves as it headed into the critical 1942 campaign season. Certainly high-quality infantry units such as 5. or 8. leichte-Division, or SS-'Totenkopf' could have been better utilized protecting AOK 6's flanks on the Don River, rather than defending marshland in the Ramushevo corridor. In truth, Hitler had made the basic strategic mistake of trying to hold onto places such as the Demyansk and Rzhev salients for reasons of prestige, rather than for sound military reasons. It was only because Stalin handed him a consolation prize by sacrificing over half a million of his troops in futile attacks at Demyansk that Hitler could view it as a tactical victory.

Typically, the Demyansk campaign is regarded as the inception of the idea that since the Luftwaffe had succeeded in supplying the encircled II AK by air, that it could repeat this effort for AOK 6. During the Demyansk airlift, Luftflotte I was

sometimes able to fly in over 300 tons of supplies per day but started with the advantage of good airfields, innovative leadership and initially weak enemy resistance in the air. Nevertheless, many members of the OKH and OKL missed the point of how difficult it was for Luftflotte I to attain the 300-tons-per-day requirement and that, even when achieved, it was providing only half of the food and ammunition actually required by II AK. At Stalingrad, Luftflotte 4 was asked to deliver 700 tons per day over a roughly similar distance, but without any of the previous advantages. Most of the Luftwaffe leadership was aware that Luftflotte I's transport fleet had never come close to 700 tons per day, but Göring – who was no longer involved with operational details – assured Hitler that it could be done. What is often missed is that the Demyansk airlift was still going on, albeit on a much smaller scale, when the Stalingrad airlift began. The Luftwaffe simply could not conduct two major airlifts simultaneously, which determined that the Demyansk campaign was no longer sustainable.

For the 13 months, between January 1942 and February 1943, over 400,000 Soviet troops and 100,000 German troops fought a protracted death struggle around the heretofore obscure town of Demyansk. An equally grim fight, ranking up there with famous last stands such as Rorke's Drift and the Alamo, was fought at the town of Kholm. Once the Soviet Winter Counteroffensive of 1941–42 succeeded in encircling II AK at Demyansk and other units at Kholm, the German Luftwaffe used its air transport force to create an air bridge to sustain the pockets until Heeresgruppe Nord could organize a relief operation in spring 1942 – a first in military history. All told, about 800,000 soldiers were killed or wounded in this protracted battle of attrition. Yet even though Demyansk was the second-longest campaign on the Eastern Front in World War II after the siege of Leningrad, it is virtually unknown today. If remembered at all, it is noted as a precedent to the Luftwaffe's later attempt to supply the trapped AOK 6 at Stalingrad in the winter of 1942–43, even though the Demyansk campaign actually ended after the Stalingrad campaign. For the Soviets, Demyansk and Kholm formed a frustrating experience of somehow snatching defeat from the jaws of victory and thus, are not worthy of significant mention in the history of the Great Patriotic War.

THE BATTLEFIELD TODAY

Although Russia has been opening up to foreign tourism its World War II battlefields for only the past 15 years or so, Demyansk, Kholm and Staraya Russa today are well off the radar screen. A trip to the region in May 2011 revealed an area that is rich in military history and local reverence for fallen heroes, but no consideration of foreign interest in these battles. There are certainly museums, monuments and military cemeteries in the region south of Lake Il'men, but the road network in the area is still sparse and hotels virtually non-existent.

En route to Staraya Russa from St Petersburg, one can see the Partisan's Glory monument just north of Luga. Soviet partisans have a number of memorials throughout the region. Heading on to Staraya Russa, the Museum of the North-western Front is well stocked with photographs and artefacts of the Demyansk campaign, including parts of shot-down Ju-52 transport planes, stacks of German identity discs and weapons dredged up from the marshes. Outside the museum, sits a T-26 light tank in pristine condition. Driving down through the former Ramushevo corridor, past endless miles of silver birch and marsh, one sees signs of defensive works still evident here and there. At Tsemena, there is a monument to 154th Naval Rifle Brigade and nearby, eroded fieldworks. On the Pola River, German concrete dragon's teeth and company-sized fighting positions still guard an important crossing site.

A reconstructed German log bunker, west of Demyansk. The Germans had the opportunity during the autumn of 1941, and then again during the summer of 1942, to build a number of stout defensive positions using the plentiful local timber. (Phil Curme)

Near Bely Bor and Kammenaya Gora (Stone Mountain), machine-gun and mortar positions from the SS-'Totenkopf' are still being found, complete with rusted ammunition and other abandoned field gear. Teams of Russian diggers, all dressed in camouflaged fatigues, are also quite noticeable and they extract both human remains and military equipment from the marshes around Demyansk. Inside Demyansk, there are more monuments to Soviet partisans as well as the Popovo Boloto POW camp, where the Germans allowed thousands of Soviet prisoners to starve to death. A large German military cemetery is located at Kupova. Both airstrips at Demyansk are overgrown and long since out of use.

Travelling farther south to Kholm, there is less direct evidence of the battle, since only one building in the town survived the siege. Nor does anything remain of the airstrip, but an open field. Yet the Lovat River still flows sluggishly through the town and there is an unusually sombre mood to the place, even by Russian standards.

TOP
A view of the Lujonka River taken from a former machine-gun position belonging to the SS-'Totenkopf' Division. The German ability to fend off most attacks is quite apparent in this photo, owing to an advantage in elevation which gave the Germans clear fields of fire and a water obstacle to slow down attackers. Just behind this position, there are the remains of a German 81mm mortar position, complete with rusted rounds still in situ. (Phil Curme)

BOTTOM
Recovery of Soviet war dead on Kamennaya Gora continues, May 2011. In the foreground are the skulls and other remains of nearly 30 Soviet soldiers killed during the Demyansk campaign. Large amounts of rusted weapons and ammunition are also recovered. Many Soviet troops were lost in the marshes and forests around Demyansk and both 'white' (legitimate) and 'black' (illegitimate) digging will continue for many more years in this area. (Phil Curme)

FURTHER READING

Primary records at NARA (partial)

Heeresgruppe Nord, Ia Reports, 15 December 1941, T311, Rolls 269–270

AOK 16, Ia Reports, Kriegstagbuch, 1 December 1941 to 31 January 1942, T312, Roll 544

    Quartermaster Reports, 22 December 1941 to 31 March 1942, T312, Roll 552

    Lagekarten, December 1941 to March 1942, T312, Roll 565

    Ic Reports, January–June 1942, T312, Rolls 567, 568, 572

II Armeekorps, Ia Reports, T314, Rolls 109–112

    Quartermaster Reports, T314, Rolls 113–116

X Armeekorps, Ia, Order of Battle, T314, Roll 459

    Ic Reports, T314, Roll 460

329. Infanterie-Division, Ia, Kriegstagbuch, December 1941 to June 1943, T315, Roll 2053

290. Infanterie-Division, Ia, Kriegstagbuch, December 1941 to February 1942, T315, Rolls 1888–1889

123. Infanterie-Division, Ia Reports, T315, Rolls 1330–1333

Secondary sources

Bartov, Omer, *The Eastern Front, 1941–45: German Troops and the Barbarization of Warfare* (New York: Macmillan, 2001)

Erickson, John, *The Road to Stalingrad* (New Haven, CT: Yale University Press, 1999)

Glantz, David M., *After Stalingrad* (Solihul, UK: Helion & Co., 2008)

——, *Forgotten Battles of the German-Soviet War, Volume II* (Self-published, 1999)

——, *Forgotten Battles of the German-Soviet War, Volume III* (Self-published, 1999)

——, *The Ghosts of Demiansk* (Self-published, 1998)

Haupt, Werner, *Demjansk 1942 – Ein Bollwerk im Osten* (Eggolsheim: Dorfler Verlag, 1963)

Isayev, Alexi V., *Наступление маршала ШапоШшникова [Marshal Shaposhnikov Offensive]* (Yauza: Penguin Books, 2005)

Kurowski, Franz, *Demjansk: Der Kessel im Eis* (Friedburg: Podzun-Pallas, 2001)

Mark, Jason D., *Besieged: The Epic Battle for Kholm* (Pymble, Australia: Leaping Horseman Books, 2011)

Morzik, Frits, *German Air Force Airlift Operations* (Honolulu: University Press of the Pacific, 2002)

Muck, Richard, *Kampfgruppe Scherer: 105 Tage eingeschlossen* (Oldenburg: Gerhard Stalling Verlag, 1943)

Perro, Oskars, *Fortress Cholm* (Toronto: Kurland Publishing, 1981)

Rutherford, Jeff, 'Life and Death in the Demyansk Pocket: The 123rd Infantry Division in Combat and Occupation', *Central European History*, Vol. 41, Issue 3, 2008, pp. 347–80

INDEX